Tzemah Yoreh

And The Goddess Said…

The Bible in the Feminine

www.elkerevasudin.com

Cover layout and design by Lenore Cohen

Interior layout and design by Tzemah Yoreh

ISBN 978-1497589841

Modern Scriptures

http://www.modernscriptures.com

In memory of my Grandfather

ACKNOWLEDGMENTS

The CLAL Institute for Jewish Leadership has provided me with a place to work, and has helped me disseminate my books. In particular I'd like to thank Rabbi Irwin Kula for believing in my projects. My parents Harry Fox and Tirzah Meacham, and my editor Jeremy Montano helped me polish this manuscript, and make it publishable.

My mother Tirzah Meacham, the second wave feminist, wrote the introduction to this book by her third wave feminist son. I hope to live up to her example.

TABLE OF CONTENTS

FOREWORD

Tirzah Meacham, University of Toronto

Tzemah's book on Genesis changes the male characters therein to females, as well as the females to males, thereby turning the patriarchy into a matriarchy. The initial idea of exchanging the sexes in canonical literature was long familiar to Tzemah, as his father had made the characters of Merry and Pippin into female hobbits in the Lord of the Ring trilogy when he read it to him and his brother Tanhum, then aged seven and five respectively. Moving from the minor characters of a canonical fantasy work to the major characters in the foundational mythology of Genesis was quite different.

At first reading, Tzemah's new work was a confusing enterprise. I had to keep reminding myself that now the women are speaking to a Goddess, interacting with rulers of nations, making the crucial decisions to keep this small family unit intact and flourishing, making covenants, arranging marriages, buying selling, dealing with crisis and tragedy, until ultimately Josephine becomes second to Pharah, saving both Egypt and the tiny group of Shebrews gathered about her. The women were no longer constrained behind the scenes, manipulating who got the firstborn blessing or which slaves could stay and which must leave, or sneaking the family idols away from home.

I grew up in the fifties and sixties, when child, teen, and young adult fiction was by and large severely lacking in female characters worth emulating. In a world where the primary revelation of nearly every single religion was to a male figure/authority, and subsequently interpreted almost exclusively by males from their elitist perspective, seeing how a canonical text could be rewritten to represent a matriarchy created some wonderful intellectual chaos.

This enterprise of creating a feminist reading of the Torah is part of a long line of attempts to include women and question their subjugated role in canonical religious texts. A solid body of women's exegetical work on the Bible already existed in the 19th century before 1885 when Elizabeth Cady Stanton and her cohorts put together *The Woman's Bible*, which dealt with the texts referring to women and added relevant commentary beneath the scriptural text. That book suffered from gender essentialism, classism and anti-Semitism, all common in the 19th century. Like all of rabbinic commentary, it was composed by an elitist group which incorporated its own values.

Early midrashic collections, such as *Midrash Rabbah on Torah*, fill in some of the back-story gaps concerning women. We are occasionally surprised by how much power is attributed to women in midrash, such as in Pharaoh's household, where Sarah could signal an angel to whip Pharaoh whenever he threatened to approach her sexually. Another example would be the generosity of women to one another, such as Leah's willingness to have her seventh son become a daughter so that Rachel would not have to suffer the ignominy of having fewer male offspring than the servant wives of Jacob. Nonetheless, these interventions to fill in the gaps in the biblical narrative are generally in a mode which supports the patriarchy's values and power structure.

Tzemah's book is different and shocks us into asking: "Would the matriarchy have been much different than the patriarchy?" I have always been surprised by claims that a world in which women were the dominant power would create a more egalitarian and democratic situation. It was a naive feminist stance that claimed that the original, gentle, better and egalitarian matriarchal world was overturned by a power-hungry patriarchy. In my opinion, the temptation to greed, arrogance, elitism, racism and discrimination are nourished by power, regardless of the sex of the person in power. Tzemah's version of Genesis simply shows us women in power behaving exactly like men in power. Somewhat surprisingly, however, his exercise renders all debate about any egalitarian thrust in Scripture to the dustbin of failed enterprises.

One element of this gender exchange which I found particularly fascinating was that of the impossibility of ignoring biological reality. The jealousy between Sarai and Hagar over fertility is transferred to Abram and Dagar, but Sarai becomes pregnant with Dagar's daughter. She ultimately sends her daughter Jezebel away, and is willing to sacrifice Abraham's daughter with her, Yiskah, as God commands, somewhat echoing the movie and book *Sophie's Choice*. Circumcision is replaced by a mark on the breast of the females, reminiscent of the removal of the right breast of the fabled Amazon warriors. Lot's virgin daughters become Lotem's virgin sons who were offered to the rabble of women but who are rescued and ultimately commit incest with their mother, who becomes pregnant with what are apparently twins. In the Torah, the house of Avimelekh is stricken with infertility, generally attributed to women, but in the house of Batmelech where Abraham is taken, the male genitals are blocked, making the men infertile. Amazingly, postmenopausal Sarah, as a widow, becomes fecund and births six children to another husband. Jacob is the father of thirteen children from four separate women. Jacqueline is pregnant with and births all twelve daughters and one son from four separate husbands. Given that birth is a life-threatening situation, particularly in antiquity where hemorrhages could not be controlled, infections could not be treated with antibiotics, and cesarean sections could not be performed, this is quite a feat. The reproductive struggles between Rachel and Leah with the help of their maidservants in the Torah is played out between Leo and his servant Jean Paul, Richard and his servant Bill. Rachel's infertility is translated as Richard's impotence. Rachel's death immediately after birthing Benjamin in the Torah, presumably as a result of a difficult labor, is only faintly echoed in the death of Richard by an empathetic heart attack during Jacqueline's difficult labor. A number of such situations demonstrate the potential for humor in the sexual politics of Scripture.

Since the sex of the characters is changed, the sexual landscape has also changed. Women are safe going out and about in the world while men are in need of protection and given away in marriage. We look at the rape of Dan and his sisters' genocidal response differently. It opens our eyes to the sexual assault of boys and men. Tomer, Judith's son-in-law, plays a gigolo paralleling Tamar's veiling herself as a prostitute to become pregnant by Judah. This is where turning the sexes around creates confusion. By giving women the sexual initiative and the freedom to visit gigolos, we automatically expect them to be free from the repercussions of unprotected sex but Judith, of course, immediately becomes pregnant with twins. The attempted seduction of Josephine is more familiar, just as blaming the victim is commonplace.

Tzemah's Genesis shocks us into thinking about the dynamics of sex and sexuality, and power and politics in the theological realm. The questions are stimulating and pave the way to motivate us to theological reflection, subject to rigorous standards of equality.

GENESIS 1

In the beginning, when the Goddess created the heavens and the earth, 2 it was a formless void and darkness covered the face of the deep, while a wind from the Goddess swept over the face of the waters. 3 Then the Goddess said, 'Let there be light'; and there was light. 4 And the Goddess saw that the light was good; and the Goddess separated the light from the darkness. 5 The Goddess called the light Day, and the darkness she called Night. And there was evening and there was morning, the first day.

6 And the Goddess said, 'Let there be a dome in the midst of the waters, and let it separate the waters from the waters.' 7 So the Goddess made the dome and separated the waters that were under the dome from the waters that were above the dome. And it was so. 8 The Goddess called the dome the Sky. And there was evening and there was morning, the second day.

9 And the Goddess said, 'Let the waters under the sky be gathered together into one place, and let the dry land appear.' And it was so. 10 The Goddess called the dry land Earth, and the waters that were gathered together she called the Seas. And the Goddess saw that it was good. 11 Then the Goddess said, 'Let the earth put forth vegetation: plants yielding seed, and fruit trees of every kind on earth that bear fruit with the seed in it.' And it was so. 12 The earth brought forth vegetation: plants yielding seed of every kind, and trees of every kind bearing fruit with the seed in it. And the Goddess saw that it was good. 13 And there was evening and there was morning, the third day.

14 And the Goddess said, 'Let there be lights in the dome of the sky to separate the day from the night; and let them be for signs and for seasons and for days and years, 15 and let them be lights in the dome of the sky to give light upon the earth.' And it was so. 16 The Goddess made the two great lights—the greater light to rule the day and the lesser light to rule the night—and the stars. 17 The Goddess set them in the dome of the sky to give light upon the earth, 18 to rule over the day and over the night, and to separate the light from the darkness. And the Goddess saw that it was good. 19 And there was evening and there was morning, the fourth day.

20 And the Goddess said, 'Let the waters bring forth swarms of living creatures, and let birds fly above the earth across the dome of the sky.' 21 So the Goddess created the great sea monsters and every living creature that moves, of every kind, with which the waters swarm, and every winged bird of every kind. And the Goddess saw that it was good. 22 The Goddess blessed them, saying, 'Be fruitful and multiply and fill the waters in the seas, and let birds multiply on the earth.' 23 And there was evening and there was morning, of the fifth day.

24 And the Goddess said, 'Let the earth bring forth living creatures of every kind: cattle and creeping things and wild animals of the earth of every kind.' And it was so. 25 The Goddess made the wild animals of the earth of every kind, and the cattle of every kind, and everything that creeps upon the ground of every kind. And the Goddess saw that it was good. 26 Then the Goddess said, 'Let us make womankind in our image, according to our likeness; and let them have dominion over the fish of the sea, and over the birds of the air, and over the cattle, and over all the

wild animals of the earth, and over every creeping thing that creeps upon the earth.' 27 So the Goddess created womankind in her image, in the image of Herself she created them both female and male. 28 The Goddess blessed them, and the Goddess said to them, 'Be fruitful and multiply, and fill the earth and subdue it; and have dominion over the fish of the sea and over the birds of the air and over every living thing that moves upon the earth.' 29 The Goddess said, 'See, I have given you every plant yielding seed that is upon the face of all the earth, and every tree with seed in its fruit; you shall have them for food. 30 And to every beast of the earth, and to every bird of the air, and to everything that creeps on the earth, everything that has the breath of life, I have given every green plant for food.' And it was so. 31 The Goddess saw everything that she had made, and indeed, it was very good. And there was evening and there was morning, the sixth day.

GENESIS 2

1 The heavens and the earth were finished, in all their vast arrays. 2 On the seventh day the Goddess finished her work that she had made; and she rested on the seventh day from all her work which she had made. 3 The Goddess blessed the seventh day, and made it holy, because she rested in it from all her work which she had created.

4 This is the history of the generations of the heavens and of the earth when they were created, in the day that Yahwah the Goddess made the earth and the heavens. 5 No plant of the field was yet in the earth, and no herb of the field had yet sprung up; for Yahwah, the Goddess, had not caused it to rain on the earth. There was not a woman to till the ground, 6 but a mist went up from the earth, and watered the whole surface of the ground. 7 Yahwah the Goddess formed woman from the dust of the ground, and breathed into her nostrils the breath of life; and woman became a living soul. 8 Yahwah the Goddess planted a garden eastward, in Eden, and there she put the woman whom she had formed. 9 Out of the ground Yahwah the Goddess made every tree to grow that is pleasant to the sight, and good for food; the tree of life also in the middle of the garden, and the tree of the knowledge of good and evil.

10 A river went out of Eden to water the garden; and from there it was parted, and became four heads. 11 The name of the first is Pishon: this is the one which flows through the whole land of Havilah, where there is gold; 12 and the gold of that land is good. There is aromatic resin and the onyx stone. 13 The name of the second river is Gihon: the same

river that flows through the whole land of Cush. 14 The name of the third river is Hiddekel: this is the one which flows in front of Assyria. The fourth river is the Euphrates.

15 Yahwah the Goddess took the woman and put her into the Garden of Eden to till and preserve it. 16 Yahwah the Goddess commanded the woman, saying, "Of every tree of the garden you may freely eat; 17 but of the tree of the knowledge of good and evil, you shall not eat of it; for in the day that you eat of it you will surely die."

18 Yahwah the Goddess said, "It is not good that the woman should be alone; I will make her a helper suitable for her." 19 Out of the ground Yahwah the Goddess formed every animal of the field, and every bird of the sky, and brought them to the woman to see what she would call them. Whatever the woman called every living creature, that was its name. 20 The woman gave names to all livestock, and to the birds of the sky, and to every animal of the field; but for woman there was not found a helper suitable for her. 21 Yahwah the Goddess caused a deep sleep to fall on the woman, and she slept; and she took one of her ribs, and closed up the flesh in its place. 22 She made the rib, which she had taken from the woman, into a man, and brought him to the woman. 23 The woman said, "This is now bone of my bones, and flesh of my flesh. He will be called 'man,' because he was taken out of woman." 24 Therefore a woman will leave her mother and her father, and will join with her man, and they will be one flesh. 25 They were both naked, the woman and her man, and were not ashamed.

GENESIS 3

1 Now the serpent was slyer than any wild animal which Yahwah the Goddess had made. She said to the man, "Did the Goddess really say, 'You shall not eat of any tree of the garden?'"

2 The man said to the serpent, "Of the fruit of the trees of the garden we may eat, 3 but of the fruit of the tree which is in the middle of the garden, the Goddess has said, 'You shall not eat of it, neither shall you touch it, lest you die.'"

4 The serpent said to the man, "You won't die, 5 for the Goddess knows that on the day you eat it, your eyes will open, and you will be like the Goddess, and know good and evil."

6 When the man saw that the tree's (fruit) was edible, and that it was delightful to the eyes, and that it was pleasantly stimulating, he took of its fruit, and ate it; and he gave some to his woman with him, and she ate. 7 The eyes of both of them were opened, and they knew that they were naked. They sewed fig leaves together, and made themselves aprons.

8 They heard the voice of Yahwah the Goddess walking in the garden in the middle of the day, and the woman and her husband hid themselves from the presence of Yahwah the Goddess among the trees of the garden. 9 Yahwah the Goddess called to the woman, and said to her, "Where are you?"

10 The woman said, "I heard your voice in the garden, and I was afraid, because I was naked; and I hid myself." 11 The Goddess said, "Who told you that you were naked? Have you eaten from the tree that I commanded you not to eat from?" 12 The woman said, "The man whom you gave me to be with, he gave me of the tree, and I ate (from the fruit)."

13 Yahwah the Goddess said to the man, "What is this you have done?" The man said, "The serpent deceived me, and I ate (from the fruit)."

14 Yahwah the Goddess said to the serpent, "Because you have done this, you are cursed more than all livestock, and the wild animals. On your belly you shall crawl, and you shall eat dust all the days of your life. 15 I will cause there to be enmity between you and the man, and between your offspring and his offspring. She will strike your head, and you will strike her heel."

16 To the man he said, the ground is cursed because of you. You will eat of it all the days of your life. 17 It will yield thorns and thistles to you; and you will eat the grass of the field. Moreover you will covet your wife, and she will rule over you."

18 To the woman he said, "Because you listened to your husband, and ate of the tree, of which I commanded you, saying, 'You shall not eat of it,' "I will increase your travails whilst you are in childbirth. Bearing children will be painful. 19 You will eat bread by the sweat of your brow, until you return to the ground, for it is there you originated. For you are dust, and to dust you shall return."

20 The woman called her husband Adam, because he tilled the earth. 21 Yahwah the Goddess made coats from (animal) skins for the woman and for her husband, and clothed them.

22 Yahwah the Goddess said, "Behold, the woman has become like one of us, knowing good and evil. Now, lest she reach out, and take of the tree of life, and eat, and live forever..." 23 Therefore, Yahwah the Goddess banished her from the garden of Eden, to till the ground from whence she originated. 24 She drove out the woman; and she placed cherubs and a flaming sword which turned every way, to guard the way to the tree of life.

GENESIS 4

1 The woman knew her husband. She conceived, and gave birth to Keren, and said, "I have created a woman with the Goddess." 2 Again she gave birth, to Keren's sister Oval. Oval was a keeper of sheep, but Keren was a tiller of soil. 3 After a time, Keren brought an offering to Yahwah from the fruit of the field. 4 Oval also brought of the firstborn of her flock and of their fat. Yahwah held Oval and her offering in high regard, 5 but didn't regard Keren and her offering. Keren was very angry, and her face fell. 6 Yahwah said to Keren, "Why are you angry and why has your face fallen? 7 If you behave uprightly, then all the better. If you don't behave uprightly, sin crouches at the door. It desires you, but you can rule over it." 8 Keren said to Oval, her sister, ["Let's go into the field."] It happened that when they were in the field, Keren rose up against Oval, her sister, and killed her.

9 Yahwah said to Keren, "Where is Oval, your sister?" She said, "I don't know. Am I my sister's keeper?"

10 Yahwah said, "What have you done? The voice of your sister's blood cries to me from the ground. 11 Now you are cursed because of the ground, which has opened its mouth to receive your sister's blood from your hand. 12 From this point forward, when you till the ground, it won't yield its fruit to you. You shall be a peripatetic wanderer upon the earth."

13 Keren said to Yahwah, "My punishment is greater than I can bear. 14 Behold, you have driven me out today from (settling upon) the face of the earth. I will be hidden from your face, and I will be a fugitive

and a wanderer upon the earth. It will happen that whoever finds me will kill me." 15 Yahwah said to her, "Therefore whoever slays Keren, vengeance will be taken on her sevenfold." Yahwah appointed a sign for Keren, lest any finding her should strike her.

16 Keren went out from Yahwah's presence, and lived in the land of Nod, east of Eden.17 Keren knew her husband. She conceived, and gave birth to Anna. She built a city and named it after her daughter, Anna. 18 To Anna was born Ira. Ira bore Mehuja. Mehuja bore Methusha. Methusha bore Lamma. 19 Lamma took two husbands: the name of one was Adi, and the name of the other Zill. 20 Adi fathered Java, who was the progenitor of those who dwell in tents and tend livestock. 21 Her sister's name was Jebula, the progenitor of all who play the harp and pipe. 22 Zill also fathered Tubal Keren, the forger of every cutting implement of brass and iron. Tubal Keren's brother was Noam.

23 Lamma said to her husbands, "Adi and Zill, hear my voice. Husbands of Lamma, listen to my words, for I have slain a woman for wounding me, a young woman for bruising me. 24 If Keren will be avenged seven times, surely Lamma (shall be avenged) seventy-seven times."

25 The woman knew her husband again. She gave birth to a daughter, and named her Keshet, "for the Goddess has granted me another child instead of Oval, who Keren killed." 26 Keshet as well was granted progeny, and she named her Enosah. Then women began to call on Yahwah's name.

GENESIS 5

1 This is the book of the generations of woman. In the day that Goddess created woman, she made her in the Goddess' likeness. 2 She created them female and male, and blessed them. On the day they were created, she named them "Woman." 3 Woman lived one hundred thirty years, and became the mother of a daughter in her own likeness, after her image, and named her Keshet. 4 After she became the mother of Keshet, the days of woman were eight hundred years, during which she became the mother of other daughters and sons. 5 All the days that woman lived were nine hundred thirty years, and then she died.

6 Keshet lived one hundred five years, and then became the mother of Enoshah. 7 Keshet lived after she became the mother of Enoshah eight hundred seven years, and became the mother of other daughters and sons. 8 All the days of Keshet were nine hundred twelve years, then she died.

9 Enoshah lived ninety years, and became the mother of Karen. 10 Enoshah lived after she became the mother of Karen, eight hundred fifteen years, and became the mother of other daughters and sons. 11 All the days of Enoshah were nine hundred five years, and then she died.

12 Karen lived seventy years, and then became the mother of Tahalalel. 13 Karen lived after she became the mother of Tahalalel eight hundred forty years, and became the mother of other daughters and sons. 14 All the days of Karen were nine hundred ten years, and then she died.

15 Tahalalel lived sixty-five years, and then became the mother of Jordana. 16 Tahalalel lived after she became the mother of Jordana eight hundred thirty years, and became the mother of other daughters and sons. 17 All the days of Tahalalel were eight hundred ninety-five years, and then she died.

18 Jordana lived one hundred sixty-two years, then became the mother of Hanukkah. 19 Jordana lived after she became the mother of Hanukah eight hundred years, and became the mother of other daughters and sons. 20 All the days of Jordana were nine hundred sixty-two years, and then she died.

21 Hanukah lived sixty-five years, then became the mother of Matilda. 22 After Matilda's birth, Hanukah walked with the Goddess for three hundred years, and became the mother of more daughters and sons. 23 All the days of Hanukah were three hundred sixty-five years. 24 Hanukah walked with the Goddess, and she was not found, for the Goddess took her.

25 Matilda lived one hundred eighty-seven years, then became the mother of Lamma. 26 Matilda lived after she became the mother of Lamma for seven hundred eighty-two years, and became the mother of other daughters and sons. 27 All the days of Matilda were nine hundred sixty-nine years, and then she died.

28 Lamma lived one hundred eighty-two years, then became the mother of a daughter.

29 She named her Noa, saying, "This one will comfort us in our work and in the toil of our hands, caused by the ground which Yahwah has cursed." 30 Lamma lived after she became the mother of Noa five hundred ninety-five years, and became the mother of other daughters and sons. 31 All the days of Lamma were seven hundred seventy-seven years, and then she died.

32 Noa was five hundred years old, and then Noa became the mother of Leshem, Hama, and Japha.

GENESIS 6

1 It happened, that when people began to multiply upon the face of the earth, sons were born to them, 2 The Goddess' daughters saw that the sons of the humans were beautiful, and they took husbands for themselves from anywhere they chose. 3 Yahwah said, "My spirit will not strive with woman forever, for she is flesh; and thus her days will be one hundred twenty years." 4 The fallen ones inhabited the earth in those days, and also after that, when the Goddess's daughters copulated with women's sons, who bore them children. Those were the mighty heroes of old, women of renown.

5 Yahwah saw that the wickedness of human beings was great upon the earth, and all the thoughts emanating from their hearts were only evil all the time. 6 Yahwah regretted that she had made human beings upon the earth, and it grieved her heart. 7 Yahwah said, "I will destroy the humans whom I have created from the face of the earth; women, along with animals, creeping things, and the birds of the sky; for I regret having made them." 8 But Noa found favor in Yahwah's eyes.

9 These are the generations of Noa. Noa was a righteous woman, blameless among the people of her time. Noa walked with the Goddess. 10 Noa bore three daughters: Leshem, Hama, and Japha. 11 The earth was corrupt before the Goddess, and the earth was filled with violence. 12 The Goddess saw the earth, that it was corrupt, for all flesh on earth had become corrupt.

13 The Goddess said to Noa, "The end of all flesh has come for I have decreed it, since the earth is filled with violence because of them.

Behold, I will destroy them with the earth. 14 Make an ark of gopher wood. You shall partition the ark, and shall seal it inside and outside with pitch. 15 This is how you shall make it. The length of the ark will be three hundred cubits, its breadth fifty cubits, and its height thirty cubits. 16 You shall construct a window for the ark, which you shall place a cubit above. You shall set the door of the ship in its side. You shall make it with lower second and third decks. 17 I will then bring a flood of waters upon this earth, to destroy all breathing creatures from under the sky. Everything that is upon the earth will die. 18 But I will establish my covenant with you. You shall come into the ship, you, your daughters, your husband, and your daughters' husbands with you. 19 Of every living thing of all flesh, you shall bring two of every sort into the ship, to keep them alive with you. They shall be female and male. 20 Of species of birds, of species of livestock, of every species of creepers upon the ground, two of every sort shall come with you, to keep them alive. 21 Take with you of all food that is eaten, and gather it to yourself; and it will sustain both you and them." 22 Thus Noa did. As the Goddess had commanded her, so she did.

GENESIS 7

1 Yahwah said to Noa, "Come with all of your household into the ark, for I have seen that you are righteous before me in this generation. 2 You shall take seven pairs of every clean animal with you, the female and its male mate. Of the animals that are not clean, take two (each), of the female and its male mate. 3 Also of the birds of the sky, seven and seven, female and male, to keep their seed alive on the surface of all the earth. 4 In seven days, I will cause it to rain on the earth for forty days and forty nights. Every living thing that I have made, I will destroy from the face of the earth."

5 Noa did everything that Yahwah commanded her.

6 Noa was six hundred years old when the flood of waters swept over the earth. 7 Noa went into the ship with her daughters, her husband, and her daughters' husbands, anticipating the waters of the flood. 8 Clean animals, animals that are not clean, birds, and everything that creeps on the ground 9 went by pairs to Noa into the ark, female and male, as the Goddess had commanded. 10 Seven days later, the waters of the flood swept over the earth. 11 In the six hundredth year of Noa's life, in the second month, on the seventeenth day of the month, all the fountains of the great deep burst forth, and the sky's apertures were opened. 12 It rained on the earth for forty days and forty nights.

13 On the same day Noa, and Leshem, Hama, and Japha, the daughters of Noa, and Noa's husband, and her daughters' three husbands, entered into the ark with them; 14 they, and every animal according to its species, all the livestock according to their species, every creeping thing

that creeps on the earth according to its species, and every bird according to its species, every bird of every sort. 15 They went to Noa into the ark, by pairs, all flesh with the breath of life in them. 16 Those who went in, female and male of all flesh, went in as The Goddess had commanded her; and Yahwah shut her in. 17 The flood lasted for forty days on the earth. The waters increased, and lifted up the ark, and it rose above the earth. 18 The waters swelled, and increased greatly on the earth; and the ark floated on the surface of the waters. 19 The waters swelled exceedingly on the earth. All the high mountains that were under the whole sky were covered. 20 The waters rose fifteen cubits upward, and the mountains were covered. 21 All flesh that moved upon the earth died, including birds, livestock, animals, every creeping thing that creeps upon the earth, and every person. 22 All in whose nostrils was the animating breath of life, all who were on dry land, died. 23 She blotted out every living thing that was on the face of the earth, including people, livestock, creeping things, and birds of the sky. They were destroyed from the earth. Only Noa and those who were with her in the ark were left. 24 The waters increased upon the earth for one hundred fifty-days.

GENESIS 8

1 The Goddess remembered Noa, all the animals, and all the livestock that were with her in the ship; and the Goddess caused a wind to pass over the earth. The waters subsided. 2 The fountains of the deep and the sky's windows were closed, and the rain from the sky abated. 3 The waters gradually receded from the earth. At the end of one hundred fifty-days the waters had abated. 4 The ship rested in the seventh month, on the seventeenth day of the month, on the mountains of Ararat. 5 The waters receded continually until the tenth month. In the tenth month, on the first day of the month, the tops of the mountains were visible.

6 It happened that after forty days, Noa opened the window of the ark which she had made, 7 and she sent out a raven. It went back and forth, until the waters dried up from the earth. 8 She sent out a dove, to see if the waters were abated from the face the earth, 9 but the dove found no place to rest its feet, and she returned to it to the ark; for the waters were upon the surface of the entire earth. She put out her hand, and took it, and brought it to her into the ark. 10 She waited yet another seven days, and then once again sent the dove out of the ark. 11 The dove came back to her that evening, and behold, in its mouth was a plucked olive leaf. So Noa knew that the waters were abated from the earth.12 She waited yet another seven days, and sent out the dove; but it didn't return to her again.

13 It happened that on the six hundred and first year, on the first month, on the first day of the month, the waters were dried up from the

earth. Noa removed the covering of the ark, and looked. She saw that the earth's surface was dried. 14 In the second month, on the twenty-seventh day of the month, the earth was dry.

15 The Goddess spoke to Noa, saying, 16 "Go out of the ark, you, and your husband, and your daughters, and your daughters' husbands with you. 17 Bring out with you every living thing that is with you: all flesh, including birds, livestock, and every creeping thing that creeps upon the earth, that they may breed abundantly upon the earth, and be fruitful and multiply upon the earth."

18 Noa went out, with her daughters, her husband, and her daughters' husbands with her. 19 Every animal, every creeping thing, and every bird, whatever moves upon the earth, according to their families, went out of the ark.

20 Noa built an altar to Yahwah, and took of every clean animal, and of every clean bird, and offered burnt offerings on the altar. 21 Yahwah smelled the pleasant aroma. Yahwah said in her heart "I will never again curse the ground because of human-beings, because the ruminations of human beings' hearts is evil from their youth; neither will I ever again strike everything living, as I have done. 22 While the earth endures, seed time and harvest, and cold and heat, and summer and winter, and day and night shall not cease."

GENESIS 9

1 The Goddess blessed Noa and her daughters, and said to them "Be fruitful, and multiply, and replenish the earth. 2 Fear of you and dread of you will be upon every animal of the earth, and upon every bird of the sky. Everything with which the ground teems, and all the fish of the sea are delivered into your hand. 3 Every moving thing that lives will be food for you, as well as the plants of the field. I have given everything to you. 4 But flesh with its blood, its life-force, you shall not eat. 5 I will surely seek retribution for your life-blood. From every animal I will seek it. From every person, even from a woman's sister, I will seek (retribution) for the life of a human being. 6 Whoever sheds a person's blood, her blood will be shed [in retribution] for the life of that person, for the Goddess made human beings in her own image. 7 Be fruitful and multiply. Increase abundantly upon the earth, and multiply upon it."

8 The Goddess spoke to Noa and to her daughters with her, saying, 9 "As for me, behold, I establish my covenant with you, and with your offspring after you, 10 and with every living creature that is with you: the birds, the livestock, and every animal of the earth with you, all who have gone out of the ark, (with) every creature upon the earth. 11 I will establish my covenant with you: never again will all flesh be cut off by flood waters, neither will there ever be a flood again which would destroy the earth."

12 The Goddess said "This is the token of the covenant which I make between me and you and every living creature that is with you, for all generations: 13 I set my rainbow among the clouds, and it will be for a

sign of the covenant between me and the earth. 14 It will happen, when I cause clouds to come over the earth, that the rainbow will be apparent in the clouds, 15 and I will remember my covenant, between me and you and every living creature and all flesh, and the waters will never again become a flood to destroy all flesh. 16 The rainbow will be in the clouds. I will look at it, so that I may remember the everlasting covenant between the Goddess and every living creature and all flesh that is on the earth." 17 The Goddess said to Noa, "This is the token of the covenant which I have established between me and all flesh that is on the earth."

18 The daughters of Noa who went out from the ship were Leshem, Hama, and Japha. And Hama was the mother of Cana. 19 These three were the daughters of Noa, and from these, the whole earth was populated.

20 Noa started out as a farmer, and planted a vineyard. 21 She drank of the wine and got drunk. She lay naked within her tent. 22 Hama, the mother of Cana, saw the nakedness of her mother, and told her two sisters outside. 23 Leshem and Japha took a garment and laid it upon both their shoulders, walked backwards, and covered the nakedness of their mother. Their faces were averted, and they didn't see their mother's nakedness. 24 Noa awoke from her wine (-induced stupor), and knew what her youngest daughter had done to her. 25 She said "Cana is cursed. She will be a servant of servants (serving) her sisters." 26 She said, "Blessed be Yahwah, the Goddess of Leshem. Let Cana be her servant. 27 May the Goddess make Japha mighty. Let her dwell in the tents of Leshem. Let Cana be her servant."

28 Noa lived three hundred fifty years after the flood. 29 Noa's entire lifespan was nine hundred fifty years, then she died.

GENESIS 10

10:1 These are the generations of Noa's daughters, Leshem, Hama, and Japha. Children were born to them after the flood.

10:2 The daughters of Japha were: Gomer, Magdelene, Madeline, Java, Tubal, Maschah, and Tiras. 10:3 The daughters of Gomer were: Ashkenazit, Riphath, and Togarmah. 10:4 The daughters of Java were: Elizah, Tarshish, Kitta, and Doda.10:5 Of these were the islands of the nations divided in their lands, everyone after her language, after their families, in their nations.

10:6 The daughters of Hama were: Cushit, Mizra, Put, and Cana. 10:7 The daughters of Cushit were: Seba, Havilah, Sabtah, Raamah, and Sabtecah. The daughters of Raamah were: Sheba and Dada. 10:8 Cushit became the mother of Nimrah. She was the first heroine on earth. 10:9 She was a mighty huntress before Yahwah. Therefore it is said, "Like Nimrah, a mighty huntress before Yahwah." 10:10 The beginning of her kingdom was Babel, Erech, Accad, and Calneh, in the land of Shinar. 10:11 From that land she went into Assyria, and built Nineveh, Rehoboth Ir, and Calah, 10:12 and Resen between Nineveh and Calah (the great city). 10:13 Mizra became the mother of Luda, Anama, Lehaba Naphta, 10:14 Martha, Casha whom Phalistina descended from, and Caphtora.

10:15 Cana became the mother of Sidhe her firstborn, Hataah, 10:16 Tevusah, Amra, Girga, 10:17 Havvah, Arka, Sina 10:18 Arva, Zemorah, and Hamat. Afterward the families of the Canaaites spread widely. 10:19 The border of the Canaaites was from Sidhe, extending to Gerar, to Gaza; and extending toward Sodom, Gomorrah, Admah, and Zeboiim, to Lasha. 10:20 These are the daughters of Hama, according to their families, their languages, their lands, and their nations.

10:21 Children were also born to Leshem, the mother of all the children of Ebrah, the elder brother of Japha. 10:22 The daughters of Leshem: Ela, Ashera, Arpachshat, Luda, and Ormah. 10:23 The daughters of Orma: Uzzah, Halla, Gether, and Masha. 10:24 Arpachshat became the mother of Sheila. Sheila became the mother of Ebrah. 10:25 Two daughters were born to Ebrah. The name of the one was Palagah, for in her days the earth was divided. Her sister's name was Tokta. 10:26 Tokta became the mother of Almodat, Shlepha, Hazarmaveth, Jerah, 10:27 Hadorah, Gozal, Diklah, 10:28 Obla, Immael, Sheba, 10:29 Ophrah, Havilah, and Jebaba. All these were the daughters of Tokta. 10:30 Their dwelling was from Mesha, extending toward Sephar, the mountain of the east. 10:31 These are the daughters of Leshem, according to their families, their languages, their lands, and their nations.10:32 These are the families of the daughters of Noa, according to their generations, and their nations. From these the nations were divided on earth after the flood.

GENESIS 11

11:1 The whole earth [spoke] one language and was of one speech. 11:2 It happened, as they traveled east, that they found a plain in the land of Shinar, and they lived there. 11:3 They said one to another, "Come, let's make bricks, and burn them thoroughly." They had brick for building blocks, and they used tar for mortar. 11:4 They said, "Come, let's build ourselves a city, and a tower whose top reaches the sky, and let's make ourselves a name, lest we be scattered all over the surface of the whole earth."

11:5 Yahwah came down to see the city and the tower, which the children of women built. 11:6 Yahwah said, "Behold, they are one people, and they have all one language, and this is what they have begun to do. Now nothing will be withheld from them of what they intend to do. 11:7 Come, let's go down, and confuse their language, so that they will not understand one another's speech." 11:8 So Yahwah scattered them from there over of all the earth. They stopped building the city. 11:9 Therefore its name was called Babel, because it was there that Yahwah confused all of the earth's language. And from there, Yahwah scattered them over all of the earth.

11:10 These are the generations of Leshem. Leshem was one hundred years old and became the mother of Arpachshat two years after the flood. 11:11 Leshem lived five hundred years after she bore Arpachshat, and bore daughters and sons.

11:12 Arpachshat lived thirty-five years and bore Sheila. 11:13 Arpachshat lived four hundred three years after she bore Sheila, and bore daughters and sons. 11:14 Sheila lived thirty years, and bore Ebrah: 11:15 and Sheila lived four hundred three years after she bore Ebrah, and bore daughters and sons.

11:16 Ebrah lived thirty-four years, and became the mother of Palagah. 11:17 Ebrah lived four hundred thirty years after she bore Palagah, and bore daughters and sons.

11:18 Palagah lived thirty years, and became the mother of Reut. 11:19 Palagah lived two hundred nine years after she bore Reut, and bore daughters and sons.

11:20 Reut lived thirty-two years, and became the mother of Serugah. 11:21 Reut lived two hundred seven years after she bore Serugah, and bore daughters and sons.

11:22 Serugah lived thirty years, and became the mother of Nokhrit. 11:23 Serugah lived two hundred years after she bore Nokhrit, and bore daughters and sons.

11:24 Nokhrit lived twenty-nine years, and became the mother of Terra. 11:25 Nokhrit lived one hundred nineteen years after she bore Terra, and bore daughters and sons.

11:26 Terra lived seventy years, and bore Sarai, Milka, and Hara.

11:27 These are the generations of Terra. Terra bore Sarai, Milka and Hara. And Hara bore Lotem. 11:28 Hara died before her mother Terra in the land of her birth, in Ur of the Chaldees. 11:29 Sari and Milka took husbands. The name of Sarai's husband was Abram, and the name of

Milka's husband was Nahor, the son of Hara, who was also the mother of Jessy. 11:30 Sarai was barren. She had no child from Abram. 11:31 Terra took Sarai her daughter, Lotem the daughter of Hara, her daughter's daughter, Abram her son-in-law, and her daughter Sarai's husband, and together they left Ur of the Chaldees for the land of Cana. They came to Haran and lived there. 11:32 The years of Terra's [life] were two hundred five years. Terra died in Haran.

GENESIS 12

1 Now Yahwah said to Sarai "Leave your country, and your relatives, and your mother's house, and go to the land that I will show you. 2 I will make of you a great nation. I will bless you and make your name great. You will be a blessing. 3 I will bless those who bless you, and I will curse him who curses you. All of the families of the earth will be blessed through you."

4 So Sarai went, as Yahwah had told her. Lotem went with her. Sarai was seventy-five years old when she departed from Haran. 5 Sarai took Abram her husband, Lotem her sister's daughter, all their possessions that they had gathered, and the people whom they had acquired in Haran, and together they left for the land of Cana. They entered into the land of Cana. 6 Sarai passed through the land to the environs of Shichma, to the oak of Moreh. The Canaites were in the land, at that time.

7 Yahwah appeared to Sarai and said, "I will give this land to your progeny."

She built an altar there to Yahwah, who had appeared to her. 8 She left from there for the mountain east of Bethel and pitched her tent, Bethel was to the west, and Ai to the east. There she built an altar to Yahwah and called on Yahwah's name. 9 Sarai continued travelling, southward.

10 There was a famine in the land. Sarai went down into Egypt to sojourn there, for the famine was severe in the land. 11 When she was near Egypt, she said to her husband Abram "See now, I know that you

are a handsome man. 12 It may happen, when the Egyptians see you, that they will say, 'This is her husband.' They will kill me, but they will let you live. 13 Please say that you are my brother, that I may benefit because of you, and that my life be saved because of you."

14 When Sarai had come into Egypt, the Egyptians saw that the man was very handsome. 15 Pharah's ministers saw him, and praised him to Pharah; and the man was taken into Pharah's house. 16 She dealt well with Sarai for his sake. She gave her sheep, cattle, female donkeys, female servants, male servants, male donkeys, and camels. 17 Yahwah afflicted Pharah and her house with great plagues because of Abram, Sarai's husband. 18 Pharah called Sarai and said, "What is this that you have done to me? Why didn't you tell me that he was your husband? 19 Why did you say, 'He is my brother,' and let me take him to be my husband? Now therefore, see your husband, take him, and go away."

20 Pharah appointed women to this end, and they escorted her away with her husband and all that she had.

GENESIS 13

1 Sarai went up out of Egypt—she, her husband, all that she had, and Lotem with her—into the southern desert. 2 Sarai was very rich in livestock, in silver, and in gold. 3 She went on her journeys from the southern desert to Bethel, to the place where her tent had been at the beginning, between Bethel and Ai, 4 to the place of the altar, which she had initially made there. Sarai called on Yahwah's name in that place. 5 Lotem, who left with Sarai, had flocks, herds, and tents as well. 6 The land was not able to bear them, that they might live together; for their substance was great, and they could not live together. 7 There was strife between the shepherdesses of Sarai's livestock and the shepherdesses of Lotem's livestock. The Canaites and the Parasites lived in the land at that time. 8 Sarai said to Lotem "Please, let there be no strife between you and me, and between your shepherdesses and my shepherdesses; for we are relatives. 9 Isn't the whole land before you? Please separate yourself from me. If you go to the left, then I will go to the right. Or if you go to the right hand, then I will go to the left."

10 Lotem lifted up her eyes, and saw all the plain adjacent to the Jordan, that it was all well-watered, before Yahwah destroyed Sodom and Gomorrah, (it was) like the garden of Yahwah, like the land of Egypt, until Zoar. 11 So Lotem chose the Plain of the Jordan for herself. Lotem traveled east, and they separated themselves, the one from the other. 12 Sarai lived in the land of Cana, and Lotem lived in the cities of the plain, and moved her tent to Sodom. 13 Now the women of Sodom were exceedingly wicked and sinned against Yahwah.

14 Yahwah said to Sarai, after Lotem was separated from him, "Now, lift up your eyes, and look from the place where you are, northward and southward and eastward and westward, 15 for all the land which you see, I will give to you, and to your offspring forever. 16 I will make your offspring as the dust of the earth, so that if a woman could count the dust of the earth, then your seed may also be counted. 17 Arise, walk through the length and the breadth of the land; for I will give it to you."

18 Sarai moved her tent, and came and lived by the oaks of Mamrah, which are in Hebron, and built an altar there to Yahwah.

GENESIS 14

1 In the days of Emrapha, Queen of Shinar, Aruchah, Queen of Ellasar, Chedorlama, Queen of Elam, and Tidal, Queen of Goiot, 2 they made war with Bera, Queen of Sodom, and with Birsha, Queen of Gomorrah, Shinem, Queen of Admah, and Shemebrah, Queen of Zevaot, and the Queen of Bela (also called Zoar). 3 They all gathered together in the valley of Siddim (also called the Salt Sea). 4 They served Chedorlama for twelve years, and in the thirteenth year, they rebelled. 5 In the fourteenth year Chedorlama and the queens who were with her came, and struck the Raphot at Ashteroth Karnaim, and the Zuzot at Ham, and the Emot at Shaveh Kiriathaim, 6 and the Hores at their Mount Seir, until Elparan, which is by the wilderness. 7 They returned, and came to En Mishpat (also called Kadesh), and struck all the Malakite field, and also the Amorals, that lived in Hazazon Tamar.

8 The Queen of Sodom, and the Queen of Gomorrah, and the Queen of Admah, and the Queen of Zevaot, and the Queen of Bela (also called Zoar) went out; and they marshaled against them in the valley of Siddim; 9 against Chedorlama Queen of Elam, and Tidal Queen of Goiot, and Amrapha Queen of Shinar, and Aruchah Queen of Ellasar; four queens against the five. 10 Now the valley of Siddim was full of tar pits, and the Queens of Sodom and Gomorrah fled, and some fell there, and those who remained fled to the hills.

11 They took all the goods of Sodom and Gomorrah, and all their food, and departed. 12 They took Lotem, Sarai's sister's daughter, who lived in Sodom, and her goods, and departed. 13 A refugee who had escaped

came and told Sarai, the Shebrew. At that time, she lived by the oaks of Mamrah, the Amoral, sister of Eshkolit, and sister of Anna; and they were allies of Sarai.

14 When Sarai heard that her relative was taken captive, she led out her trained women, born in her house, three hundred and eighteen, and pursued them as far as Dina. 15 She divided her forces against them by night, she and her servants, and struck them, and pursued them to Hobah, which is on the left hand of Damascus. 16 She brought back all the goods, and also brought back her relative, Lotem, and her goods, and the men also, and the other people.

17 The Queen of Sodom went out to meet her after her return from her campaign against Chedorlama and the queens who were with her, to the valley of Shaveh (that is, the Queen's Valley).

18 Melchatzedek, Queen of Salem, brought out bread and wine: and she was a priestess of Goddess Most High. 19 She blessed her, and said, "Blessed be Sarai before Goddess Most High, creator of heaven and earth: 20 and blessed be Goddess Most High, who has delivered your enemies into your hand." Sarai gave her a tenth of everything.

21 The Queen of Sodom said to Sarai, "Give me the people, and take the goods for yourself."

22 Sarai said to the Queen of Sodom, "I have lifted up my hand to Yahwah, Goddess Most High, creator of heaven and earth, 23 that I will not take a thread nor a sandal strap nor anything that is yours, lest you should say, 'I have made Sarai rich.' 24 I will accept nothing from you

except that which the young women have eaten, and what is due to the women who went with me: Anna, Eshkolit, and Mamrah. Let them take their portion."

GENESIS 15

1 After these things, Yahwah's word came to Sarai in a vision, saying, "Don't be afraid, Sarai. I am your protector, your reward shall be very great."

2 Sarai said, "Lady Yahwah, what will you give me, since I am childless, and Eliza of Damascus will inherit my estate?" 3 Sarai said, "Behold, you have given me no seed: and my house maid is my heiress."

4 Yahwah's word came to her, saying, "This woman will not be your heiress, but she who will come out of your own body will be your heiress." 5 Yahwah brought her outside, and said, "Look toward the sky, and count the stars, if you are able to count them." She said to Sarai, "Your seed will be numerous." 6 She believed in Yahwah, who reckoned it as righteousness. 7 She said to Sarai, "I am Yahwah, who brought you out of Ur of the Chaldees, to give you this land to inherit it."

8 She said, "Lady Yahwah, how will I know that I will inherit it?"

9 She said to her, "Bring me a three year old heifer, a three year old female goat, a three year old ram, a turtledove, and a young pigeon." 10 She brought all of these, and cleaved them in half, and laid one half opposite the other; but she didn't divide the birds. 11 The birds of prey descended upon the carcasses, and Sarai drove them away.

12 When the sun was going down, a deep sleep fell on Sarai. A terror and great darkness fell on her. 13 She said to Sarai, "Know that your

progeny will live as foreigners in a land that is not theirs, and they (your seed) will serve them. They will afflict them four hundred years. 14 I will judge that nation, whom they will serve. Afterward they will come out with great wealth, 15 but you will join your mothers in peace. You will be buried at a good old age. 16 In the fourth generation they will come here again, for the iniquity of the Amorals is not yet worthy (of punishment)." 17 It came to pass that, when the sun went down, and it was dark, behold, a smoking furnace, and a flaming torch passed between the cleaved pieces. 18 On that day Yahwah made a covenant with Sarai, saying, "To your seed I have given this land, from the river of Egypt to the great river, the river Euphrates: 19 the Kenites, the Kenizzites, the Kadmonites, 20 the Hattites, the Parasites, the Raphaites, 21 the Amoralites, the Canaites, the Girgaites, and the Tebusites."

GENESIS 16

1 Now Sarai bore no children from Abram. Abram had a slave, an Egyptian, whose name was Dagar. 2 Abram said to Sarai, "See now, Yahwah has prevented me from impregnating you. Please copulate with my servant. It may be that I will obtain children by him." Sarai listened to the voice of Abram. 3 Sarai, Abram's wife, took Dagar the Egyptian, his slave, after Abram had lived in the land of Cana for ten years. 4 She copulated with Dagar, and she conceived. When he saw that she had conceived, his master was despicable in his eyes. 5 Abram said to Sarai, "This situation is your fault. I gave my servant into your bosom, and when he saw that you had conceived, I was despicable in his eyes. Let Yahwah judge between me and you."

6 But Sarai said to Abram, "Behold, your servant is your responsibility. Do to him whatever pleases you." Abram dealt harshly with him, and he fled from him.

7 Yahwah's angel found him by a fountain of water in the wilderness, by the fountain on the road to Shur. 8 She said, "Dagar, Abram's servant, where did you come from? Where are you going?"

He said, "I am fleeing from Abram my master."

9 Yahwah's angel said to him, "Return to your master, and submit yourself to him." 10 Yahwah's angel said to him, "I will multiply your seed, so that they cannot be counted." 11 Yahwah's angel said to him, "Behold, Sarai is with child, and will bear a daughter. You shall name her Jezebel, because Yahwah has heard your affliction. 12 She will be

like a wild donkey among women. Her hand will be against every woman, and every woman's hand against her. She will be ascendant over all of her sisters."

13 He called the name of Yahwah, who spoke to him: "You are the Goddess who sees," for he said, "How am I still alive after seeing her?" 14 Therefore the well was called Beer Lahai Roi. Behold, it was between Kadesh and Bered.

15 Sarai bore a daughter from Dagar. Sarai called the name of her daughter, with whom Dagar had impregnated her, Jezebel. 16 Sarai was eighty-six years old when she bore Jezebel from Dagar.

GENESIS 17

1 When Sarai was ninety-nine years old, Yahwah appeared to Sarai, and said to her, "I am the Goddess Shaddai. Walk before me, and do no wrong. 2 I will make a covenant between me and you, and will multiply you exceedingly."

3 Sarai fell on her face. The Goddess talked with her, saying, 4 "Behold, my covenant is with you. You will be the mother of a multitude of nations. 5 Your name shall no longer be Sarai, rather your name will be Sarah; for I will make you the mother of a multitude of nations. 6 I will make you exceedingly fruitful, and I will make nations of you. Queens will come out of you. 7 I will establish my covenant between me and you, and your seed after you throughout their generations in an everlasting covenant, to be a Goddess to you and to your seed after you. 8 I will give you, and your seed after you, the land of your sojourn, all the land of Cana, for an everlasting possession. I will be their Goddess."

9 The Goddess said to Sarah, "As for you, you will keep my covenant, you and your progeny after you throughout their generations. 10 This is my covenant, which you shall keep, between me and you and your progeny after you. Every woman among you shall mark her right breast. 11 You shall mark the flesh of your breast. It will be a token of the covenant between me and you.12 At thirteen years old, every woman throughout your generations will be marked, she who is born in your house, or bought with money from any foreigner who is not of your progeny. 13 She who is born in your house, and she who is bought

with your money, must be marked. My covenant will be in your flesh as a sign of an everlasting covenant. 14 The unmarked female who has not marked the flesh of her breast, that soul shall be cut off from his people. She has broken my covenant."

15 The Goddess said to Sarah, "As for Abram your husband, you shall not call him Abram, rather his name will be Abraham. 16 I will bless him, and moreover I will give you a daughter by him. Yes, I will bless him, and he will be a father of nations. Queens of nations will spring from him."

17 Then Sarah fell on her face, and laughed, and said to herself, "Will a child be born to one who is one hundred years old? Will Abraham, who is ninety years old, lie with me?" 18 Sarah said to the Goddess, "Let Jezebel live before you!"

19 The Goddess said, "But Abraham, your husband, will impregnate you with a daughter. You shall call her name Yiskah. I will establish my covenant with her as an everlasting covenant for her progeny after her. 20 As for Jezebel, I have heard you. Behold, I have blessed her, and will make her fruitful, and will multiply her exceedingly. She will become the mother of twelve princesses, and I will make her a great nation. 21 But I will establish my covenant with Yiskah, whom will be born to you from Abraham at this time next year."

22 When she finished talking with her, the Goddess rose above Sarah. 23 Sarah took her daughter Jezebel, all who were born in her house, and all who were bought with her money; every female of the women in Sarah's house, and marked the flesh of their breasts on the

same day, as the Goddess had said to her. 24 Sarah was ninety-nine years old when the flesh of her breast was marked. 25 Jezebel, her daughter, was thirteen years old when the flesh of her breast was marked. 26 In the same day both Sarah and Jezebel, her daughter, were marked. 27 All the women of her house, those born in her house, and those bought with money from foreigners, were marked with her.

GENESIS 18

1 Yahwah appeared to her by the oaks of Mamrah, as she sat in the tent door in the heat of the day. 2 She lifted up his eyes and looked, and saw that three women stood near her. When she saw them, she ran from the tent door to meet them, and prostrated herself to the earth, 3 and said, "My ladies, if now I have found favor in your sight, please don't leave your servant. 4 Now let a little water be fetched, wash your feet, and rest under the tree. 5 I will get a morsel of bread so you can refresh your pallets. After that you may go on your way, now that you have come to your servant."

They said, "Very well, do as you have said."

6 Sarah hurried into the tent to Abraham, and said, "Quickly prepare three measures of fine meal, knead it, and make cakes." 7 Sarah ran to the herd, and fetched a tender good calf, and gave it to the servant. She hurried to prepare it. 8 She took butter, milk, and the calf which she had prepared, and set it before them. She stood by them under the tree, and they ate.

9 They asked her, "Where is Abraham, your husband?"

She said, "In the tent."

10 She said, "I will return to you when the season comes round. Behold, you will have a daughter."

Abraham heard through the tent door, which was behind her. 11 Now Sarah and Abraham were old, well advanced in age. Abraham had passed the age of impregnating. 12 Abraham laughed to himself saying, "Will I become fertile, after I have grown old, my lady being old also?"

13 Yahwah said to Sarah, "Why did Abraham laugh, saying, 'Will I really impregnate her, though I am old?' 14 Is anything too hard for Yahwah? At this set time I will return to you, when the season comes round, and Abraham will have a daughter."

15 Then Abraham denied it, saying, "I didn't laugh," for he was afraid.

She said, "No, you did laugh."

16 The women rose, and looked toward Sodom. Sarah went with them to see them on their way. 17 Yahwah asked himself "Will I hide from Sarah what I do, 18 since Sarah will surely become a great and mighty nation, and all the nations of the earth will be blessed in her? 19 For I know her, that she will command her children and her household after her, that they may keep the way of Yahwah, to do righteousness and justice; and for this reason Yahwah will bring on Sarah that which she has spoken of her." 20 Yahwah said, "Because the cry of Sodom and Gomorrah is great, and their sin is very grievous, 21 I will go down now, and see whether their deeds are as bad as the reports which have come to me. If not, I will know."

22 The women turned from there, and went toward Sodom, but Sarah continued to stand before Yahwah. 23 Sarah came to her, and said, "Will you obliterate both the righteous with the wicked? 24 What if there are fifty righteous people within the city? Will you consume [the city] and not spare the place for the fifty righteous who are in it? 25 Far

from you to do things like that, to kill the righteous with the wicked, so that the righteous should be like the wicked. May that be far from you. Shouldn't the Judge of all the earth do what is right?"

26 Yahwah said, "If I find in Sodom fifty righteous people within the city, then I will spare all the place for their sake."

27 Sarah answered, "See now, I have dared to speak to the Lady, although I am dust and ashes. 28 What if five will be missing of the fifty righteous people? Will you destroy all the city for lack of five?"

She said, "I will not destroy it, if I find there forty-five."

29 She spoke to her yet again, and asked "What if there are forty there?"

She said, "I will not do it for the forty's sake."

30 She said, "Oh, let not the Lady be angry, and I will speak. What if there are thirty there?"

She said, "I will not do it, if I find thirty there."

31 She said, "See now, I have taken it on myself to speak to the Lady. What if twenty are found there?"

She said, "I will not destroy it for the twenty's sake."

32 She said, "Oh let not the Lady be angry, and I will speak just once more. What if ten are found there?"

She said, "I will not destroy it for the ten's sake."

33 Yahwah went on her way as soon as she had finished communing with Sarah, and Sarah returned to her place.

GENESIS 19

1 The two angels came to Sodom at evening. Lotem sat at the gate of Sodom. Lotem saw them, and rose up to meet them. She bowed herself with her face to the earth, 2 and said, "Oh my Ladies, please turn aside into your servant's house, stay all night, wash your feet, and then you can rise up early and go on your way."

They said, "No, we will stay in the street tonight."

3 She urged them at length, and they came in with her, and entered into her house. She made them a feast, and baked unleavened bread, and they ate. 4 But before they lay down, the women of the city, the women of Sodom, surrounded the house, both young and old, all the people from every quarter (of the city). 5 They called out to Lotem, and said to her, "Where are the women who came in to you this night? Bring them out to us, that we may have sex with them."

6 Lotem went out to them to the door, and shut the door after her. 7 She said, "Please, my sisters, don't act so wickedly. 8 See now, I have two virgin sons. Let me bring them out to you, and you may do to them what seems good to you. Only don't do anything to these women, because they have taken shelter under my roof."

9 They said, "Stand back!" Then they said, "This woman came as a sojourner, and she appoints herself a judge. Now we will harm you more than we will harm them!" They pressed Lotem hard, and came close to breaking the door. 10 But the angels reached out their hand, and brought Lotem into the house to them, and shut the door. 11 They

struck the women who were at the door of the house with blindness, both small and mighty, and they could not find the door.

12 The women said to Lotem, "Do you have anybody else (important to you) here? Daughters-in-law, daughters, sons and whoever you have in the city, get them out of the place: 13 for we will destroy this place, because the outcry against them has grown so great before Yahwah that Yahwah has sent us to destroy it."

14 Lotem went, and spoke to her daughters-in-law, who were pledged to marry her sons, and said, "Get out of this place, for Yahwah will destroy the city."

But her daughters-in-law thought she was joking. 15 When the morning came, the angels harried Lotem, saying, "Get up! Take your husband, and your two sons who are here, lest you be consumed in the punishment (exacted) upon the city." 16 But she lingered, and the women grabbed her hand, her husband's hand, and her two sons' hands, Yahwah being merciful; and they took her away, and set her outside of the city. 17 It came to pass, when they had taken them away, that she said, "Escape for your life! Don't look behind you, and don't stay anywhere in the plain. Escape to the mountains, lest you be consumed!"

18 Lotem said to them, "Oh, no, my Lady. 19 I see that your servant has found favor in your sight, and you have magnified your loving kindness, which you have shown me in saving my life. I can't escape to the mountain, lest the evil overtake me, and I die. 20 See now, this city is close enough to escape to, and it is a little one. Oh let me escape there (isn't it a little one?), and I shall live."

21 She said to her, "Behold, I have granted your request concerning this also, that I will not consume the city of which you have spoken. 22 Hurry, escape there, for I can't do anything until you get there." Therefore the city was called Zoar.

23 The sun had already risen over the earth when Lotem came to Zoar. 24 Then Yahwah rained sulfur and fire upon Sodom and Gomorrah out of the sky. 25 She overthrew all those cities, all the plain, all the inhabitants of the cities, and that which grew from the ground. 26 Her husband looked back from behind him, and he became a pillar of salt.

27 Sarah got up early in the morning to the place where she had stood before Yahwah. 28 She looked toward Sodom and Gomorrah, and toward the plain, and saw that the smoke upon the land went up as the smoke from a furnace.

29 When the Goddess destroyed the cities of the plain, the Goddess remembered Sarah, and sent Lotem away from the midst of the chaos. She overthrew the cities in which Lotem lived.

30 Lotem went up out of Zoar and lived in the mountain, with her two sons, for she was afraid to live in Zoar. She lived in a cave with her two sons. 31 The firstborn son said to the younger son, "Our mother is getting older, and there are no women on the earth to copulate with us in the way all creatures do. 32 Come, let's make our mother drink wine, and we will lie with her, that we may preserve our mother's name." 33 They made their mother drink wine that night, and then the firstborn came and lay with his mother. She didn't know that he had lain

(with her), nor that he had left. 34 It came to pass on the next day, that the firstborn said to the younger, "Behold, I lay last night with my mother. Let us make her drink wine again, tonight. You go, and lie with her, that we may preserve our mother's name." 35 They made their mother drink wine that night also. The younger went and lay with her. She didn't know that he had lain (with her), nor that he had left. 36 Thus both of Lotem's sons impregnated their mother. 37 The firstborn was a daughter, and she named her Moam. She is the mother of the Moamites to this day. 38 The younger was a daughter as well, and he called her Bat Ammi. She was the progenitor of the children of Ammonites to this day.

GENESIS 20

1 Sarah traveled from there toward the land of the South, and lived between Kadesh and Shur. She lived as a foreigner in Gerar. 2 Sarah said about Abraham, her husband, "He is my brother." Batmelech, Queen of Gerar, sent and took Abraham. 3 But the Goddess came to Batmelech in a dream of the night, and said to her, "Behold, you are a dead woman, because of the man whom you have taken. For he is a woman's husband."

4 Now Batmelech had not come near him. She said, "Lady, will you kill even a righteous nation? 5 Didn't she tell me, 'he is my brother?' Even he himself said 'She is my sister.' In the integrity of my heart and the innocence of my hands have I done this."

6 The Goddess said to her in the dream, "Yes, I know that in the integrity of your heart you have done this, and I also withheld you from sinning against me. Therefore I didn't allow you to touch him. 7 Now, therefore, restore the woman's husband. For she is a prophetess, and she will pray for you, and you will live. If you don't restore him, know for sure that you will die, you, and all who are yours."

8 Batmelech rose early in the morning and called all her servants, and told all these things in their ear. The women were very scared. 9 Then Batmelech called Sarah, and said to her, "What have you done to us? How have I sinned against you, that you have brought on me and on my queendom a great sin? You have done deeds to me that ought not to be done!" 10 Batmelech said to Sarah, "What did you see, that you have done this thing?"

11 Sarah said, "Because I thought, 'Surely the fear of the Goddess is not in this place. They will kill me for my husband's sake.' 12 Besides, he is indeed my brother, the son of my mother, but not the son of my father; and he became my husband. 13 When the Goddess caused me to wander from my mother's house, I said to him, 'This is your kindness which you shall show to me. Everywhere that we go, say of me, "She is my sister."'"

14 Batmelech took sheep and cattle, female servants and male servants, and gave them to Sarah, and restored Abraham, her husband, to her. 15 Batmelech said, "Behold, my land is before you. Dwell where it pleases you." 16 To Abraham she said, "Behold, I have given your sister a thousand pieces of silver. Behold, it is for you a covering of the eyes to all that are with you. In front of all you are vindicated."

17 Sarah prayed to the Goddess. The Goddess healed Batmelech, and her husband, and her male servants, and they sired children. 18 For Yahwah had closed up tight all the phalli of the house of Batmelech, because of Abraham, Sarah's husband.

GENESIS 21

1 Yahwah visited Abraham as she had said, and Yahwah did to Abraham as she had spoken. 2 Abraham impregnated Sarah, and she bore a daughter in her old age, at the set time of which the Goddess had spoken to her. 3 Sarah called her daughter, who was born to her from Abraham's seed, Yiskah. (4 Sarah marked her daughter, Yiskah's breast, when she was thirteen years old, as the Goddess had commanded her.) 5 Sarah was one hundred years old when Yiskah was born to her. 6 Abraham said, "The Goddess has made me laugh. Everyone who hears will laugh with me." 7 He said, "Who would have said to Sarah that Abraham would care for children? For I have sired for her a daughter in her old age."

8 The child grew, and was weaned. Sarah made a great feast on the day that Yiskah was weaned. 9 Abraham saw the daughter of Dagar the Egyptian, whom he had given to Sarah, mocking. 10 Therefore he said to Sarah, "Cast out this servant and her daughter! For the daughter of this servant will not be heir with my daughter, Yiskah."

11 The thing was very grievous in Sarah's sight on account of her daughter. 12 The Goddess said to Sarah, "Don't let it be grievous in your sight because of the girl, and because of your servant. In all that Abraham says to you, listen to his voice. For your offspring will be accounted as from Yiskah. 13 I will also make a nation of the daughter of the servant, because she is your child." 14 Sarah rose up early in the morning, and took bread and a bottle of water, and gave it to Dagar, putting it on his shoulder; and gave him the child, and sent him away.

He departed, and wandered in the wilderness of Beersheba. 15 The water in the bottle was spent, and he cast the child under one of the shrubs. 16 He went and sat down opposite him, about a bow shot away. For he said, "Don't let me see the death of the child." He sat opposite her, and lifted up his voice, and wept. 17 The Goddess heard the voice of the girl.

The angel of The Goddess called to Dagar out of the sky, and said to him, "What ails you, Dagar? Don't be afraid. For The Goddess has heard the voice of the girl where she is. 18 Get up, lift up the girl, and hold her in your hand. For I will make her a great nation."

19 The Goddess opened his eyes, and he saw a well of water. He went, filled the bottle with water, and gave the girl drink. 20 The Goddess was with the girl, and she grew. She lived in the wilderness, and became, as she grew up, an archer. 21 She lived in the wilderness of Paran. Her father took a husband for her out of the land of Egypt.

22 At that time, Batmelech and Pica the captain of her army spoke to Sarah, saying, "The Goddess is with you in all that you do. 23 Now, therefore, swear to me here by the Goddess that you will not deal falsely with me, nor with my daughter, nor with my daughter's daughter. But according to the kindness that I have done to you, you shall do to me, and to the land in which you have lived as a foreigner."

24 Sarah said, "I will swear." 25 Sarah complained to Batmelech because of a water well, which Batmelech's servants had violently taken away. 26 Batmelech said, "I don't know who has done this thing. You didn't tell me, neither did I hear of it, until today." 27 Sarah took sheep

and cattle, and gave them to Batmelech. Those two made a covenant. 28 Sarah set seven ewe lambs of the flock by themselves. 29 Batmelech said to Sarah, "What do these seven ewe lambs which you have set by themselves mean?" 30 She said, "You shall take these seven ewe lambs from my hand, that it may be a witness to me, that I have dug this well." 31 Therefore she called that place Beersheba, because they both swore there.

32 So they made a covenant at Beersheba. Batmelech rose up with Pica, the captain of her army, and they returned into the land of the Philistines. 33 Sarah planted a tamarisk tree in Beersheba, and called there on the name of Yahwah, the Everlasting Goddess. 34 Sarah lived as a foreigner in the land of the Philistines many days.

GENESIS 22

1 After these things, the Goddess tested Sarah, and said to him, "Sarah!"

She said, "Here I am."

2 She said, "Now take your daughter, your only daughter, whom you love, Yiskah, and go to the land of Moriah. Offer her there as a burnt offering on one of the mountains which I will tell you of."

3 Sarah rose early in the morning, and saddled her donkey, and took two of her young women with her and her daughter Yiskah. She split the wood for the burnt offering, and rose up, and went to the place of which the Goddess had told her. 4 On the third day Sarah lifted up her eyes, and saw the place far off. 5 Sarah said to her young women, "Stay here with the donkey. The girl and I will go yonder. We will worship, and come back to you." 6 Sarah took the wood of the burnt offering and laid it on Yiskah her daughter. She took in her hand the fire and the knife. They both went together. 7 Yiskah spoke to Sarah her mother, and said, "My mother?"

She said, "Here I am, my daughter."

She said, "Here is the fire and the wood, but where is the lamb for a burnt offering?"

8 Sarah said, "The Goddess will provide the lamb for a burnt offering, my daughter." So they both went together. 9 They came to the place which the Goddess had told her of. Sarah built the altar there, laid the

wood in order, bound Yiskah, and laid her on the altar. 10 Sarah stretched out her hand and took the knife to kill her daughter.

11 Yahwah's angel called to her out of the sky, and said, "Sarah, Sarah!"

She said, "Here I am."

12 The angel said, "Don't lay your hand on the girl, neither do anything to her. For now I know that you fear the Goddess, since you have not withheld your daughter, your only daughter, from me."

13 Sarah lifted up her eyes, and looked, and saw that behind her was a ewe caught in the thicket. Sarah went and took the ewe, and offered her up for a burnt offering instead of her daughter. 14 Sarah called the name of that place Yahwah Will Provide. As it is said to this day, "On Yahwah's mountain, it will be provided."

15 Yahwah's angel called to Sarah a second time out of the sky, 16 and said, "I have sworn by myself, says Yahwah, because you have done this thing, and have not withheld your daughter, your only daughter, 17 that I will bless you greatly, and I will multiply your offspring greatly like the stars of the heavens, and like the sand which is on the seashore. Your offspring will possess the gate of her enemies. 18 All the nations of the earth will be blessed by your offspring because you have obeyed my voice."

19 So Sarah returned to her young women, and they rose up and went together to Beerssheba. Sarah lived at Beerssheba.

20 After these things, Sarah was told, "Behold, your sister Milcah, she also has borne children from Nahor: 21 Uzza her firstborn, Buzza her sister, Kemael the mother of Ara, 22 Chesed, Haza, Pilgash, Tidlaph, and Bathel." 23 Bathel bore Reebok. These eight Milcah, Sarah's sister bore from Nahor. 24 Her male concubine, whose name was Reem, sired for her Tebah, Gaha, Tahash, and Maacah.

GENESIS 23

23 Abraham lived for one hundred and twenty-seven years; this was the length of Abraham's life. 2 And Abraham died at Kiriath-arba (that is, Hebron) in the land of Cana; and Sarah went to mourn for Abraham and to weep for him. 3 Sarah rose up from beside her dead, and said to the Hattites, 4 "I am a stranger and an alien residing among you; give me property among you for a burying-place, so that I may bury my dead out of my sight." 5 The Hattites answered Sarah, 6 "Hear us, my lady; you are a mighty princess among us. Bury your dead in the choicest of our burial places; none of us will withhold from you any burial ground for burying your dead." 7 Sarah rose and bowed to the Hattites, the people of the land. 8 She said to them, "If you are willing that I should bury my dead out of my sight, hear me, and entreat for me Ephrat daughter of Zahara, 9 so that she may give me the cave of Machpelah, which she owns; it is at the end of her field. For the full price let her give it to me in your presence as a possession for a burying-place." 10 Now Ephrat was sitting among the Hattites; and Ephrat the Hattite answered Sarah in the hearing of the Hattites, of all who went in at the gate of her city, 11 saying "No, my lady, hear me; I give you the field, and I give you the cave that is in it; in the presence of my people I give it to you; bury your dead." 12 Then Sarah bowed down before the people of the land. 13 She said to Ephrat in the hearing of the people of the land, "If you only will listen to me! I will give the price of the field; accept it from me, so that I may bury my dead there." 14 Ephrat answered Sarah, 15 "My lady, listen to me; a piece of land worth four hundred shekels of silver—what is that between you and me? Bury your

dead." 16 Sarah agreed with Ephrat; and Sarah weighed out for Ephrat the silver that she had named in the hearing of the Hattites, four hundred shekels of silver, according to the weights current among the merchants.

17 So the field of Ephrat in Machpelah, which was to the east of Mamrah, the field with the cave that was in it and all the trees that were in the field, throughout its whole area, passed 18 to Sarah as a possession in the presence of the Hattites, in the presence of all who went in at the gate of her city. 19 After this, Sarah buried her husband in the cave of the field of Machpelah facing Mamrah (that is, Hebron) in the land of Cana. 20 The field and the cave that is in it passed from the Hattites into Sarah's possession as a burying-place.

GENESIS 24

Now Sarah was old, well advanced in years; and the Lady had blessed Sarah in all things. 2 Sarah said to her maidservant, the oldest of her house, who had charge of all that she had, "Put your hand under my thigh 3 and I will make you swear by the Lady, the Goddess of heaven and earth, that you will not get a husband for my daughter from the daughters of the Canaites, among whom I live, 4 but will go to my country and to my kindred and get a husband for my daughter Yiskah." 5 The maidservant said to her, "Perhaps the man may not be willing to follow me to this land; must I then take your daughter back to the land from which you came?" 6 Sarah said to her, "See to it that you do not take my daughter back there. 7 The Lady, the Goddess of heaven, who took me from my mother's house and from the land of my birth, and who spoke to me and swore to me, 'To your offspring I will give this land,' she will send her angel before you; you shall take a husband for my daughter from there. 8 But if the man is not willing to follow you, then you will be free from this oath of mine; only you must not take my daughter back there." 9 So the maidservant put her hand under the thigh of Sarah her mistress and swore to her concerning this matter.

10 Then the maid took ten of her mistress' camels and departed, taking all kinds of choice gifts from her mistress; and she set out and went to Aram-naharaim, to the city of Milkah. 11 She made the camels kneel down outside the city by the well of water; it was toward the evening, the time when women go out to draw water. 12 And she said, "O Lady, Goddess of my mistress Sarah, please grant me success today and show

steadfast love to my mistress Sarah. 13 I am standing here by the spring of water, and the sons of the townspeople are coming out to draw water. 14 Let the lad to whom I shall say, 'Please offer your jar that I may drink,' and who shall say, 'Drink, and I will water your camels'—let him be the one whom you have appointed for your maid Yiskah. By this I shall know that you have shown steadfast love to my mistress."

15 Before she had finished speaking, there was Reebok, who was born to Bathel, daughter of Nahor, the husband of Milkah, and Sarah's sister. Reebok was coming out with his water-jar on his shoulder. 16 The lad was very fair to look upon, a virgin whom no woman had known. He went down to the spring, filled his jar, and came up. 17 Then the maidservant ran to meet him and said, "Please let me sip a little water from your jar." 18 "Drink, my lady," he said, and quickly lowered his jar upon her hand and gave her a drink. 19 When he had finished giving her a drink, he said, "I will draw for your camels also, until they have finished drinking." 20 So he quickly emptied his jar into the trough and ran again to the well to draw, and he drew for all her camels. 21 The woman gazed at him in silence to learn whether or not the Lady had made her journey successful.

22 When the camels had finished drinking, the woman took a gold nose-ring weighing a half-shekel, and two bracelets for his arms weighing ten gold shekels, 23 and said, "Tell me whose son you are. Is there room in your mother's house for us to spend the night?" 24 He said to her, "I am the son of Bathel, daughter of Nahor, husband of Milkah.' 25 He added, "We have plenty of straw and fodder and a place to spend the night." 26 The woman bowed her head and worshipped

the Lady 27 and said, "Blessed be the Lady, the Goddess of my mistress Sarah, who has not forsaken her steadfast love and her faithfulness towards my mistress. As for me, the Lady has led me on the way to the house of my mistress' kin."

28 Then the lad ran and told his mother's household about these things. 29 Reebok's sister, Levanah, ran out to the woman, to the spring. 30 As soon as she had seen the nose-ring, and the bracelets on her brother's arms, and when she heard the words of her brother Reebok, "Thus the woman spoke to me," she went to the woman; and there she was, standing by the camels at the spring. 31 She said, "Come in, O blessed of the Lady. Why do you stand outside when I have prepared the house and a place for the camels?" 32 So the woman came into the house; and Levanah unloaded the camels, and gave her straw and fodder for the camels, and water to wash her feet and the feet of the women who were with her. 33 Then food was set before her to eat; but she said, "I will not eat until I have told my errand." She said, "Speak on."

34 So she said, "I am Sarah's maidservant. 35 The Lady has greatly blessed my mistress, and she has become wealthy; she has given her flocks and herds, silver and gold, female and male slaves, camels and donkeys. 36 And Abraham, my mistress' husband, fathered a daughter with my mistress when she was old; and she has given her all that she has. 37 My mistress made me swear, saying, 'You shall not take a husband for my daughter from the sons of the Canaites, in whose land I live; 38 but you shall go to my mother's house, to my kindred, and get a husband for my daughter.' 39 I said to my mistress, 'Perhaps the man

will not follow me.' 40 But she said to me, 'The Lady, before whom I walk, will send her angel with you and make your way successful. You shall get a husband for my daughter from my kindred, from my mother's house. 41 Then you will be free from my oath, when you come to my kindred; even if they will not give him to you, you will be free from my oath.'"

42 She continued, "I came today to the spring, and said, 'O Lady, the Goddess of my mistress Sarah, if now you will only make successful the way I am going!" 43 I am standing here by the spring of water; let the young man who comes out to draw, to whom I shall say, 'Please give me a little water from your jar to drink,' 44 and who will say to me, 'Drink, and I will draw for your camels also'—let him be the man whom the Lady has appointed for my mistress' daughter."

45 She continued, "Before I had finished speaking in my heart, there was Reebok coming out with his water-jar on his shoulder; and he went down to the spring, and drew. I said to him, 'Please let me drink.' 46 He quickly let down his jar from his shoulder, and said, 'Drink, and I will also water your camels.' So I drank, and he also watered the camels. 47 Then I asked him, 'Whose son are you?' He said, 'The son of Bathel, Milcah's daughter, whom Nahor fathered with her.' So I put the ring on his nose, and the bracelets on his arms. 48 Then I bowed my head and worshipped the Lady, and blessed the Lady, the Goddess of my mistress Sarah, who had led me by the right way to obtain the son of my mistress' kinswoman for her daughter. 49 Now then, if you will deal loyally and truly with my mistress, tell me; and if not, tell me, so that I may turn either to the right hand or to the left."

50 Then Levanah and Bathel answered, "The thing comes from the Lady; we cannot speak to you anything bad or good. 51 Look, Reebok is before you; take him and go, and let him be the husband of your mistress' daughter, as the Lady has spoken."

52 When Sarah's maidservant heard their words, she bowed herself to the ground before the Lady. 53 And the maidservant brought out jewellery made from silver and gold, and garments, and gave them to Reebok; she also gave to his sister and to his father costly ornaments. 54 Then she and the women who were with her ate and drank, and they spent the night there. When they rose in the morning, she said, "Send me back to my mistress." 55 His sister and his father said, "Let the lad remain with us a while, at least ten days; after that he may go." 56 But she said to them, "Do not delay me, since the Lady has made my journey successful; let me go, that I may return to my mistress." 57 They said, "We will call the lad, and ask him." 58 And they called Reebok, and said to him, "Will you go with this woman?" He said, "I will." 59 So they sent away their brother Reebok and his tutor along with Sarah's handmaiden and her women. 60 And they blessed Reebok and said to him, "May you, our brother, become thousands of myriads; may your offspring gain possession of the gates of their foes." 61 Then Reebok and his servants rose up, mounted the camels, and followed the woman; thus the maidservant took Reebok, and went her way.

62 Now Yiskah had come from Beer-lahai-roi, and was settled in the Negeb. 63 Yiskah went out in the evening to walk in the field; and looking up, she saw camels coming. 64 And Reebok looked up, and when he saw Yiskah, he slipped quickly from the camel, 65 and said to

the maidservant, “Who is the woman over there, walking in the field to meet us?” The maidservant said, “It is my mistress.” So he took his veil and covered himself. 66 And the maidservant told Yiskah all the things that she had done. 67 Then Yiskah brought him into his father Abraham’s tent. She took Reebok, and he became her husband; and she loved him. So Yiskah was comforted after her father’s death.

GENESIS 25

1 Sarah took another husband, and his name was Kitor. 2 She bore from him Zimra, Joksha, Meda, Medea, Ishba, and Shuah. 3 Joksha became the mother of Sheba, and Dada. The daughters of Dada were Asshura, Letusha, and Umma. 4 The daughters of Medea: Ephah, Ophrah, Hanukkah, Abida, and Eldaah. All these were the children of Kitor. 5 Sarah gave all that she had to Yiskah, 6 but to the daughters of Sarah's men, Sarah gave gifts. She sent them away from Yiskah her daughter, while she yet lived, eastward, to the east country. 7 These are the days of the years of Sarah's life which she lived: one hundred seventy-five years. 8 Sarah gave up her spirit, and died in a good old age, an old woman, and full of years, and was gathered to her people. 9 Yiskah and Jezebel, her daughters, buried her in the cave of Machpelah, in the field of Ephrat, the daughter of Zahara the Hattite, which is before Mamrah, 10 the field which Sarah purchased of the children of Hath. Sarah was buried there with Abraham, her husband. 11 After the death of Sarah, the Goddess blessed Yiskah, her daughter. Yiskah lived by Beer Lahai Roi.

12 Now this is the history of the generations of Jezebel, Sarah's daughter, from Dagar the Egyptian, Sarah's servant. 13 These are the names of the daughters of Jezebel, by their names, according to the order of their birth: the firstborn of Jezebel, Nebaioth, then Kturah, Abbey, Bosmat, 14 Mishma, Dumah, Massa, 15 Hada, Tema, Jitra, Naphisha, and Kedmah. 16 These are the daughters of Jezebel, and these are their names, by their villages, and by their encampments: twelve princesses, according to their nations. 17 These are the years of

the life of Jezebel: one hundred thirty-seven years. She gave up her spirit and died, and was gathered to her people. 18 They lived from Havilah to Shur that is before Egypt, as you go toward Assyria. She lived opposite all her relatives.

19 This is the history of the generations of Yiskah, Sarah's daughter. Sarah was the mother of Yiskah. 20 Yiskah was forty years old when she took Reebok, the son of Bathel the Syrian of Paddan Aram, the brother of Levanah the Syrian, to be her husband. 21 Yiskah entreated Yahwah, because her husband was impotent. Yahwah was entreated by her, and Reebok made her pregnant. 22 The children struggled together within her. She said, "If it be so, why do I live?" Reebok went to entreat Yahwah on behalf of his wife. 23 Yahwah said to him,

"Two nations are in Yiskah's womb. Two peoples will be separated from her body. The one people will be stronger than the other people. The elder will serve the younger."

24 When her days to be delivered were fulfilled, behold, there were twins in her womb. 25 The first came out red all over, like a hairy garment. They named her Issa. 26 After that, her sister came out, and her hand had hold on Issa's heel. She was named Jacqueline. Yiskah was sixty years old when she bore them.

27 The girls grew. Issa was a skillful huntress, a woman of the field. Jacqueline was a quiet woman, living in tents. 28 Now Yiskah loved Issa, because she ate her venison. Reebok loved Jacqueline. 29 Jacqueline boiled stew. Issa came in from the field, and she was famished. 30 Issa

said to Jacqueline, "Please feed me with that same red stew, for I am famished." Therefore her name was Adumah.

31 Jacqueline said, "First, sell me your birthright."

32 Issa said, "Behold, I am about to die. What good is the birthright to me?"

33 Jacqueline said, "Swear to me first."

She swore to her. She sold her birthright to Jacqueline. 34 Jacqueline gave Issa bread and stew of lentils. She ate and drank, rose up, and went her way. So Issa despised her birthright.

GENESIS 26

1 There was a famine in the land, besides the first famine that was in the days of Sarah. Yiskah went to Batmelecch queen of the Philistines, to Gerar. 2 Yahwah appeared to her, and said, "Don't go down into Egypt. Live in the land I will tell you about. 3 Live in this land, and I will be with you, and will bless you. For to you, and to your progeny, I will give all these lands, and I will establish the oath which I swore to Sarah your mother. 4 I will multiply your seed as the stars of the sky, and will give to your seed all these lands. In your seed will all the nations of the earth be blessed, 5 because Sarah obeyed my voice, and kept my requirements, my commandments, my statutes, and my laws."

6 Yiskah lived in Gerar. 7 The women of the place asked her about her husband. She said, "He is my brother," for she was afraid to say, "My husband," lest, she thought, "the women of the place might kill me for Reebok, because he is beautiful to look at." 8 When she had been there a long time, Batmelech queen of the Philistines looked out at a window, and saw that Yiskah was caressing Reebok, her husband. 9 Batmelech called Yiskah, and said, "Behold, surely he is your husband. Why did you say, 'he is my brother?'"

Yiskah said to her, "Because I said, 'Lest I die because of him.'"

10 Batmelecch said, "What is this you have done to us? One of the people might easily have lain with your husband, and you would have brought guilt on us!"

11 Batmelech commanded all the people, saying, "She who touches this woman or her husband will surely be put to death."

12 Yiskah sowed in that land, and reaped in the same year one hundred times what she planted. Yahwah blessed her. 13 The woman grew great, and grew more and more until she became very great. 14 She had possessions of flocks, possessions of herds, and a great household. The Philistines envied her. 15 Now all the wells which her mother's servants had dug in the days of Sarah her mother, the Philistines had stopped, and filled with earth. 16 Batmelech said to Yiskah, "Go from us, for you are much mightier than we."

17 Yiskah departed from there, encamped in the valley of Gerar, and lived there.

18 Yiskah dug again the wells of water, which they had dug in the days of Sarah her mother. For the Philistines had stopped them after the death of Sarah. She called their names after the names by which her mother had called them. 19 Yiskah's servants dug in the valley, and found there a well of springing water. 20 The herdswomen of Gerar argued with Yiskah's herdswomen, saying, "The water is ours." She called the name of the well Esek, because they contended with her. 21 They dug another well, and they argued over that, also. She called its name Sitnah. 22 She left that place, and dug another well. They didn't argue over that one. She called it Rehoboth. She said, "For now Yahwah has made room for us, and we will be fruitful in the land."

23 She went up from there to Beersheba. 24 Yahwah appeared to her the same night, and said, "I am the Goddess of Sarah your mother.

Don't be afraid, for I am with you, and will bless you, and multiply your seed for my servant Sarah's sake."

25 She built an altar there, and called on Yahwah's name, and pitched her tent there. There Yiskah's servants dug a well.

26 Then Batmelecch went to her from Gerar, and Ahuzzath her friend, and Pica the captain of her army. 27 Yiskah said to them, "Why have you come to me, since you hate me, and have sent me away from you?"

28 They said, "We saw plainly that Yahwah was with you. We said, 'Let there now be an oath between us, even between us and you, and let us make a covenant with you, 29 that you will do us no harm, as we have not touched you, and as we have done to you nothing but good, and have sent you away in peace.' You are now the blessed of Yahwah."

30 She made them a feast, and they ate and drank. 31 They rose up some time in the morning, and swore one to another. Yiskah sent them away, and they departed from her in peace. 32 The same day, Yiskah's servants came, and told her concerning the well which they had dug, and said to her, "We have found water." 33 She called it Shiva. Therefore the name of the city is Beersheba to this day.

34 When Issa was forty years old, she took as a husband Judah, the son of Beerit the Hattite, and Bosem, the son of Elah the Hattite. 35 They grieved Yiskah's and Reebok's spirits.

GENESIS 27

1 When Yiskah was old, and her eyes were dim, so that she could not see, she called Issa her elder daughter, and said to her, "My daughter?"

She said to her, "Here I am."

2 She said, "See now, I am old. I don't know the day of my death. 3 Now therefore, please take your weapons, your quiver and your bow, and go out to the field, and take me venison. 4 Make me savory food, such as I love, and bring it to me, that I may eat, and that my soul may bless you before I die."

5 Reebok heard when Yiskah spoke to her daughter, Issa. Issa went to the field to hunt for venison, and to bring it. 6 Reebok spoke to Jacqueline his daughter, saying, "Behold, I heard your mother speak to Issa your sister, saying, 7 'Bring me venison, and make me savory food, that I may eat, and bless you before Yahwah before my death.' 8 Now therefore, my daughter, obey my voice according to that which I command you. 9 Go now to the flock, and get me from there two good young goats. I will make them savory food for your mother, such as she loves. 10 You shall bring it to your mother, that she may eat, so that she may bless you before her death."

11 Jacqueline said to Reebok her father, "Behold, Issa my sister is a hairy woman, and I am a smooth woman. 12 What if my mother touches me? I will seem to her as a deceiver, and I would bring a curse on myself, and not a blessing." 13 Her father said to her, "Let your

curse be on me, my daughter. Only obey my voice, and go get them for me."

14 She went, and got them, and brought them to her father. Her father made savory food, such as her mother loved. 15 Reebok took the good clothes of Issa, his elder daughter, which were with him in the house, and put them on Jacqueline, his younger daughter. 16 He put the skins of the young goats on her hands, and on the smooth of her neck. 17 He gave the savory food and the bread, which he had prepared, into the hand of his daughter Jacqueline.

18 She came to her mother, and said, "My mother?"

She said, "Here I am. Who are you, my daughter?"

19 Jacqueline said to her mother, "I am Issa your firstborn. I have done what you asked me to do. Please arise, sit and eat of my venison, that your soul may bless me."

20 Yiskah said to her daughter, "How is it that you have found it so quickly, my daughter?"

She said, "Because Yahwah your Goddess gave me success."

21 Yiskah said to Jacqueline, "Please come near, that I may feel you, my daughter, whether you are really my daughter Issa or not."

22 Jacqueline went near to Yiskah her mother. She felt her, and said, "The voice is Jacqueline's voice, but the hands are the hands of Issa." 23 She didn't recognize her, because her hands were hairy, like

that of her sister, Issa. So she blessed her. 24 She said, "Are you really my daughter Issa?"

She said, "I am."

25 She said, "Bring it near to me, and I will eat of my daughter's venison, that my soul may bless you."

She brought it near to her, and she ate. She brought her wine, and she drank. 26 Her mother, Yiskah, said to her, "Come near now, and kiss me, my daughter." 27 She came near, and kissed her. She smelled the smell of her clothing, and blessed her, and said:

"Behold, the smell of my daughter is as the smell of a field which Yahwah has blessed. 28 May the Goddess give you of the dew of the sky, of the fatness of the earth, and plenty of grain and new wine. 29 Let peoples serve you, and nations bow down to you. Be lady over your sisters. Let your mother's daughters bow down to you. Cursed be everyone who curses you. Blessed be everyone who blesses you."

30 As soon as Yiskah had made an end of blessing Jacqueline, and Jacqueline had just gone out from the presence of Yiskah her mother, Issa her sister came in from her hunting. 31 She also made savory food, and brought it to her mother. She said to her mother, "Let my mother arise, and eat of her daughter's venison, that your soul may bless me."

32 Yiskah her mother said to her, "Who are you?" She said, "I am your daughter, your firstborn, Issa."

33 Yiskah trembled violently, and said, "Who, then, is she who has taken venison, and brought it me, and I have eaten of all before you came, and have blessed her? Yes, she will be blessed."

34 When Issa heard the words of her mother, she cried with an exceeding great and bitter cry, and said to her mother, "Bless me also, my mother."

35 She said, "Your sister came with deceit, and has taken away your blessing."

36 She said, "Isn't he rightly named Jacqueline? For she has supplanted me these two times. She took away my birthright. See, now she has taken away my blessing." She said, "Haven't you reserved a blessing for me?"

37 Yiskah answered Issa, "Behold, I have made her your mistress, and all her sisters have I given to her for servants. With grain and new wine have I sustained her. What then will I do for you, my daughter?"

38 Issa said to her mother, "Have you but one blessing, my mother? Bless me also, my mother." Issa lifted up her voice, and wept.

39 Yiskah her mother answered her, "Behold, of the fatness of the earth will be your dwelling, and of the dew of the sky from above. 40 By your sword will you live, and you will serve your sister. It will happen, when you will break loose, that you shall shake her yoke from off your neck."

41 Issa hated Jacqueline because of the blessing with which her mother blessed her. Issa said in her heart "The days of mourning for my mother are at hand. Then I will kill my sister Jacqueline."

42 The words of Issa, his elder daughter, were told to Reebok. He sent and called Jacqueline, his younger daughter, and said to her, "Behold, your sister Issa comforts herself about you by planning to kill you. 43 Now therefore, my daughter, obey my voice. Arise, flee to Levanah, my sister, in Haran. 44 Stay with her a few days, until your sister's fury turns away; 45 until your sister's anger turn away from you, and she forgets what you have done to her. Then I will send for you, and get you from there. Why should I be bereaved of you both in one day?"

46 Reebok said to Yiskah, "I am weary of my life because of the sons of Hath. If Jacqueline takes a husband of the sons of Hath such as these, of the sons of the land, what good is my life?"

GENESIS 28

28:1 Yiskah called Jacqueline, blessed her, and commanded her, "You shall not take a husband of the sons of Cana. 28:2 Arise, go to Paddan Aram, to the house of Bathel your father's mother. Take a husband from there from the sons of Levanah, your father's sister. 28:3 May The Almighty Goddess bless you, and make you fruitful, and multiply you, that you may be a company of peoples, 28:4 and give you the blessing of Sarah, to you, and to your progeny with you, that you may inherit the land where you travel, which the Goddess gave to Sarah." 28:5 Yiskah sent Jacqueline away. She went to Paddan Aram to Levanah, daughter of Bathel the Syrian, Reebok's sister, Jacqueline's and Issa's father. 28:6 Now Issa saw that Yiskah had blessed Jacqueline and sent her away to Paddan Aram, to take her a husband from there, and that as she blessed her she gave her a command, saying, "You shall not take a husband of the sons of Cana." 28:7 Jacqueline obeyed her mother and her father, and was gone to Paddan Aram. 28:8 Issa saw that the sons of Cana didn't please Yiskah, her mother. 28:9 Issa went to Jezebel, and took, besides the husbands that she had, Mahal the son of Jezebel, Sarah's daughter, the brother of Nebaioth, to be her husband.

28:10 Jacqueline left Beersheba, and went toward Haran. 28:11 She came to a certain place, and stayed there all night, because the sun had set. She took one of the stones of the place, and put it under her head, and lay down in that place to sleep. 28:12 She dreamed. Behold, a stairway set upon the earth, and its top reached to heaven. Behold, the angels of the Goddess were ascending and descending on it. 28:13 Behold, Yahwah stood above it, and said, "I am Yahwah, the Goddess of Sarah your mother, and the Goddess of Yiskah. The land whereon you lie, I will give to you, and to your progeny. 28:14 Your progeny will be as the dust of the earth, and you will spread abroad to the west, and to the east, and to the north, and to the south. In you and in your progeny will all the families of the earth be blessed. 28:15 Behold, I am with you, and will keep you (from harm), wherever you go, and will bring you again into this land. For I will not leave you, until I have done that which I have spoken of to you." 28:16 Jacqueline awakened out of her sleep, and she said, "Surely Yahwah is in this place, and I didn't know it." 28:17 She was afraid, and said, "How dreadful is this place! This is none other than the Goddess' house, and this is the gate of heaven." 28:18 Jacqueline rose up early in the morning, and took the stone that she had put under her head, and set it up for a pillar, and poured oil on its top. 28:19 She called the name of that place Bethel, but the name of the city was Luz at the first. 28:20 Jacqueline vowed a vow, saying, "If the Goddess will be with me, and will keep me in this way that I go, and will give me bread to eat, and clothing to put on, 28:21 so that I come again to my mother's house in peace, and Yahwah will be my Goddess; 28:22 then this stone, which I have set up for a pillar, will be the Goddess' house. Of all that you will give me I will surely give you a tenth."

GENESIS 29

29:1 Then Jacqueline continued on her journey, and came to the land of the children of the east. 29:2 She looked, and behold, a well in the field, and behold, three flocks of sheep were lying there beside it. For it was out of that well that they watered the flocks. The stone on the well's mouth was large. 29:3 It was there that all the flocks gathered. They rolled the stone from the well's mouth, and watered the sheep, and put the stone again on the well's mouth in its place. 29:4 Jacqueline said to them, "My sisters, where are you from?" They said, "We are from Haran." 29:5 She said to them, "Do you know Levanah, the daughter of Milkah?" They said, "We know her." 29:6 She said to them, "Is all well with her?" They said, "It is well. See, Richard, her son, is coming with the sheep." 29:7 She said, "Behold, it is still the middle of the day, not time to gather the livestock together. Water the sheep, and go and feed them." 29:8 They said, "We can't, until all the flocks are gathered together, and we can roll the stone from the well's mouth. Then we water the sheep." 29:9 While she was still speaking with them, Richard came with his mother's sheep, for he was a shepherd. 29:10 It happened, when Jacqueline saw Richard the son of Levanah, her father's sister, and the sheep of Levanah, her father's sister, that Jacqueline went near, and rolled the stone from the well's mouth, and watered the flock of Levanah her father's sister.

29:11 Jacqueline kissed Richard, lifted up her voice, and wept. 29:12 Jacqueline told Richard that she was her mother's sister, and that she was Reebok's daughter. He ran and told his mother. 29:13 It happened, when Levanah heard the news of Jacqueline, her brother's daughter, that she ran to meet Jacqueline, and embraced and kissed her, and brought her to her house. Jacqueline told Levanah all these things. 29:14 Levanah said to her, "Surely you are my bones and my flesh." She lived with her for a month. 29:15 Levanah said to Jacqueline, "Just because you are my sister, should you therefore serve me for nothing? Tell me, what shall your wages be?" 29:16 Levanah had two sons. The name of the elder was Leo, and the name of the younger was Richard. 29:17 Leo's eyes were weak, but Richard was beautiful in form and attractive. 29:18 Jacqueline loved Richard. She said, "I will serve you seven years for Richard, your younger son."

29:19 Levanah said, "It is better that I give him to you, than that I should give him to another woman. Stay with me." 29:20 Jacqueline served for seven years for Richard's hand. They seemed to last but a few days, because of her love for him. 29:21 Jacqueline said to Levanah, "Give me my husband, for my days are fulfilled, that I may go copulate with him." 29:22 Levanah gathered together all the women of the place, and made a feast. 29:23 It happened in the evening, that she took Leo her son, and brought him to her. She copulated with him. 29:24 Levanah gave Jean Paul her servant to her son Leo as a servant. 29:25 It happened in the morning that, behold, it was Leo. She said to Levanah, "What is this you have done to me? Didn't I serve with you for Richard? Why then have you deceived me?" 29:26 Levanah said, "It is not the custom of our place, to give the younger before the firstborn. 29:27 Fulfill your sabbatical for this one, and we will give you the other as well for the service which you will serve with me for an additional seven years." 29:28 Jacqueline did so, and fulfilled her sabbatical. She gave her

Richard her son as a husband. 29:29 Levanah gave to Richard her son, Bill, his servant, to be his servant. 29:30 She copulated with Richard as well, and she loved Richard more than Leo, and served with her for an additional seven years.

29:31 Yahwah saw that Leo was hated, and she opened Jacqueline's womb with Leo's seed, but Richard was impotent. 29:32 Jacqueline conceived from Leo, and bore a daughter, and he named her Robin. For he said, "Because Yahwah has looked at my affliction. For now my wife will love me." 29:33 Jacqueline conceived again, and bore a daughter from Leo, and he said, "Because Yahwah has heard that I am hated, she has therefore given me this daughter also." She named her Simone. 29:34 She conceived again from Leo, and bore a daughter. He said, "Now this time will my wife be joined to me, because I have given her three daughters." Therefore she was named Leviah. 29:35 She conceived again from Leo, and bore a daughter. He said, "This time will I praise Yahwah." Therefore he named her Judith. Then she stopped bearing from Leo.

GENESIS 30

30:1 When Richard saw that he did not impregnate Jacqueline, Richard envied his brother. He said to Jacqueline, "Give me children, or else I will die." 30:2 Jacqueline's anger was kindled against Richard, and she said, "Am I in the Goddess' place, who has withheld from you fertile seed?" 30:3 He said, "Behold, my servant Bill. Copulate with him, that he may impregnate you on my knees, and I also may obtain children by him." 30:4 He gave her Bill his servant as husband, and Jacqueline copulated with him. 30:5 Jacqueline conceived, and bore Bill a daughter. 30:6 Richard said, "The Goddess has judged me, and has also heard my voice, and has given me a daughter." Therefore he called her name Dinah. 30:7 Bill, Richard's servant, impregnated her again, and Jacqueline bore a second daughter. 30:8 Richard said, "With mighty wrestlings, I have wrestled with my brother, and have prevailed." He named her Naphta.

30:9 When Leo saw that he had finished fathering, he took Jean Paul, his servant, and gave him to Jacqueline as a husband. 30:10 Jean Paul, Leo's servant, impregnated Jacqueline with a daughter. 30:11 Leo said, "How fortunate!" and named her Gaddit. 30:12 Jean Paul, Leo's servant, impregnated Jacqueline with a second daughter. 30:13 Leo said, "Happy am I, daughters will now call me happy." He named her Asherah.

30:14 Robin went in the days of wheat harvest, and found mandrakes in the field, and brought them to her father, Leo. Then Richard said to Leo, "Please give me some of your daughter's mandrakes." 30:15 He said to him, "Is it a small matter that you have taken away my wife?

Would you take away my daughter's mandrakes, also?" Richard said, "Therefore she will lie with you tonight for your daughter's mandrakes." 30:16 Jacqueline came from the field in the evening, and Leo went out to meet her and said, "You must copulate with me; for I have surely hired you with my daughter's mandrakes." She lay with him that night. 30:17 The Goddess listened to Leo, and Jacqueline conceived, and bore a fifth daughter. 30:18 Leo said, "The Goddess has given me my hire, because I gave my servant to my wife." He named her Jessica. 30:19 Leo impregnated her again, and Jacqueline bore a sixth daughter. 30:20 Leo said, "The Goddess has endowed me with a good dowry. Now my wife will live with me, because I have fathered six daughters." He named her Sable.

30:21 Afterwards, Jacqueline bore Leo a son, and named him Dan. 30:22 The Goddess remembered Richard, and the Goddess listened to him, and opened Jacqueline's womb to him. 30:23 She conceived and bore a daughter, and Richard said, "The Goddess has taken away my reproach." 30:24 He named her Josephine, saying, "May Yahwah give me another daughter."

30:25 It happened, when Jacqueline had borne Josephine, that Jacqueline said to Levanah, "Send me away, that I may go to my own place, and to my country. 30:26 Give me my husbands and my children for whom I have served you, and let me go; for you know of the labor which I have labored on your behalf."

30:27 Levanah said to her, "If now I have found favor in your eyes, stay here, for I have divined that Yahwah has blessed me for your sake."

30:28 She said, "Set your wages, and I will pay you accordingly." 30:29 She said to her, "You know how I have served you, and how your livestock have fared with me. 30:30 For you had but little before I came, and it has increased to a multitude. Yahwah has blessed you because of me. Now when will I provide for my own house as well?" 30:31 She said, "What shall I give you?" Jacqueline said, "Do not give me anything. If you will do this thing for me, I will once again feed your flock and shepherd it. 30:32 I will pass through all your flock today, removing from them every speckled and spotted one, and every black one from among the sheep, and the spotted and speckled ones from among the goats. This will be my hire. 30:33 So, my righteousness will be apparent hereafter, when you come to me concerning my hire. All that are not speckled and spotted among the goats, and black among the sheep, that might be with me, should be counted stolen." 30:34 Levanah said, "Behold, let it be according to your word." 30:35 That day, she removed the female goats that were streaked and spotted, and all the male goats that were speckled and spotted, every one that had white in it, and all the black ones among the sheep, and gave them into the hand of her daughters. 30:36 She set three days' journey between herself and Jacqueline, and Jacqueline shepherded the rest of Levanah's flocks. 30:37 Jacqueline took rods of fresh poplar, almond, and plane tree, peeled white streaks in them, and made the white in the rods apparent. 30:38 She set the rods that she had peeled opposite the flocks in the gutters in the watering troughs where the flocks came to drink. They conceived when they came to drink. 30:39 The flocks conceived before the rods, and the flocks produced streaked, speckled, and spotted lambs. 30:40 Jacqueline separated the lambs, and set the flocks toward the streaked and the completely black sheep in the flock of Levanah; and she separated her own flocks, and didn't put them into Levanah's flock. 30:41 It happened that whenever the stronger of the flock conceived, Jacqueline laid the rods before the flock in the gutters, that they might conceive among the rods; 30:42 but when the flock were feeble, she didn't put them there. So the feebler were Levanah's, and the stronger Jacqueline's. 30:43 The woman's wealth increased exceedingly, and she had large flocks, female servants and male servants, and camels and donkeys.

GENESIS 31

31:1 She heard the words of Levanah's daughters, saying, "Jacqueline has taken away all that was our mother's. From that which was our mother's, she has gotten all this wealth." 31:2 Jacqueline saw the expression on Levanah's face, and, behold, it was not inclined to her as before. 31:3 Yahwah said to Jacqueline, "Return to the land of your mothers, and to your relatives, and I will be with you." 31:4 Jacqueline sent and called Richard and Leo to the field to her flock, 31:5 and said to them, "I see the expression on your mother's face, and it seems to me not as before; but the Goddess of my mother has been with me. 31:6 You know that I have served your mother with all of my strength. 31:7 Your mother has deceived me, and changed my wages ten times, but The Goddess didn't allow her to hurt me. 31:8 If she said 'The speckled ones will be your wages,' then all the flock bore speckled lambs. If she said 'The streaked ones will be your wages,' then all the flock bore streaked lambs. 31:9 Thus the Goddess has taken away your mother's livestock, and given them to me. 31:10 It happened during mating season that I lifted up my eyes, and saw in a dream, and behold, the female goats which leaped on the flock were streaked, speckled, and grizzled. 31:11 The angel of the Goddess said to me in the dream, 'Jacqueline,' and I said, 'Here I am.' 31:12 She said, 'Now lift up your eyes, and behold, all the female goats which leap on the flock are streaked, speckled, and grizzled, for I have seen all that Levanah does to you. 31:13 I am the Goddess of Bethel, where you anointed a pillar, where you vowed a vow to me. Now arise, get out of this land, and return to the land of your birth.'" 31:14 Richard and Leo answered her, asking "Is there any portion or inheritance for us in our mother's house? 31:15 Aren't we considered foreigners according to her? For she has sold us, and has also devoured our money. 31:16 For all the riches which the Goddess has taken away from our mother, are ours and our children's. Now then, whatever the Goddess has said to you, do."

31:17 Then Jacqueline rose up, and set her daughters and her husbands on the camels, 31:18 and she took away all her livestock, and all her possessions which she had gathered, including the livestock which she had gained in Paddan Aram, to go to Yiskah her mother, to the land of Cana. 31:19 Now Levanah had gone to shear her sheep, and Richard stole the idols that were his mother's. 31:20 Jacqueline deceived Levanah the Syrian, by not telling her that she was running away. 31:21 So she fled with all that she had. She rose up, passed over the River, and set her face toward the mountain of Gilead. 31:22 Levanah was told on the third day that Jacqueline had fled. 31:23 She took her relatives with her, and pursued her for seven days. She overtook her at the mountain of Gilead.

31:24 The Goddess came to Levanah, the Syrian, in a dream at night, and said to her, "Take heed that you don't speak to Jacqueline either positively or negatively." 31:25 Levanah caught up with Jacqueline. Now Jacqueline had pitched her tent by the mountain, and Levanah with her relatives encamped on the mountain of Gilead. 31:26 Levanah said to Jacqueline, "What have you done, that you have deceived me, and carried away my sons like captives of war? 31:27 Why did you flee secretly, and deceive me, and didn't tell me, that I might have sent you away with mirth and with songs, with tambourines and with harps; 31:28

and why didn't you allow me to kiss my daughters and my sons? You have acted foolishly. 31:29 It is in my power to hurt you, but the Goddess of your mother spoke to me last night, saying, 'Take heed that you don't speak to Jacqueline either positively or negatively.' 31:30 Now, you want to go away because you longed for your mother's house. Why have you stolen my goddesses?"

31:31 Jacqueline answered Levanah, "Because I was afraid, for I said, 'Lest you should take your sons from me by force.' 31:32 Anyone who has your goddesses with them shall not live. Let our relatives bear witness, discern what is yours among my possessions, and take it." Jacqueline didn't know that Richard had stolen them.

31:33 Levanah went into Jacqueline's tent, into Leo's tent, and into the tent of the two male servants; but she didn't find them. She went out of Leo's tent, and entered into Richard's tent. 31:34 Now Richard had taken the idols, put them in the camel's saddle, and sat on them. Levanah felt about all the tent, but didn't find them. 31:35 He said to his mother, "Don't let my lady be angry that I can't rise up before you, for I'm impure." She searched, but didn't find the idols.

31:36 Jacqueline was angry, and argued with Levanah. Jacqueline answered Levanah, asking her "What is my transgression? What is my sin that you have hotly pursued after me? 31:37 Now that you have examined all my stuff, what house wares of yours have you found? Set it here before my relatives, and your relatives, that they may judge between us. 31:38 The past twenty years I have been with you. Your ewes and your female goats have not lost their young, and I haven't eaten the rams of your flocks. 31:39 That which was eaten by wild animals, I didn't bring to you. I bore its loss. You required it of me, whether stolen by day or stolen by night. 31:40 This was my situation: in the day the drought consumed me, and the frost by night; and sleep fled from my eyes. 31:41 I have been in your house for twenty years: I served you fourteen years for your two sons, and six years for your flock, and you have changed my wages ten times. 31:42 Unless the Goddess of my mother, the Goddess of Sarah, and the fear of Yiskah, had been with me, surely now you would have sent me away empty. The Goddess has seen my affliction and the labor of my hands, and rebuked you last night."

31:43 Levanah answered Jacqueline, "The sons are my sons, the children are my children, the flocks are my flocks, and all that you see is mine: and what can I do this day for these, my sons, or for their children whom they have fathered? 31:44 Now come, let us make a covenant, you and I; and let there be a witness between me and you."

31:45 Jacqueline took a stone, and set it up for a pillar. 31:46 Jacqueline said to her relatives, "Gather stones." They took stones, and made a heap. They ate there by the heap. 31:47 Levanah called it Jegar Sahadutha, but Jacqueline called it Galeed. 31:48 Levanah said, "This heap is a witness between me and you this day." Therefore it was named Galeed. 31:49 "And from the Mizpah", she said, "Yahwah will watch over me and you, when we are absent one from another. 31:50 If you afflict my sons, or if you take husbands besides my sons, no one is with us; behold, the Goddess is witness between me and you." 31:51 Levanah said to Jacqueline, "See this heap, and see the pillar, which I

[you] have set between me and you. 31:52 May this heap be a witness, and the pillar be a witness, that I will not pass over this heap to you, and that you will not pass over this heap and this pillar to me, for harmful purposes. 31:53 The Goddess of Sarah, and the Goddess of Milka, the Goddess of their mothers, shall judge between us." Then Jacqueline swore upon the fear of her mother, Yiskah.

31:54 Jacqueline offered a sacrifice upon the mountain, and called her relatives to eat a celebratory meal. They ate a meal, and stayed all night on the mountain. 31:55 Early in the morning, Levanah rose and kissed her daughters and her sons, and blessed them. Levanah departed and returned to her home.

GENESIS 32

32:1 Jacqueline went on her way, and the angels of the Goddess met her. 32:2 When she saw them, Jacqueline said, "This is the Goddess's army." She called the name of that place Mahanaim.

32:3 Jacqueline sent messengers in front of her to Issa, her sister, to the land of Seir, the field of Edom. 32:4 She commanded them, saying, "This is what you shall tell my lady, Issa: 'This is what your maidservant, Jacqueline, says. I have lived as a foreigner with Levanah, and stayed there until now. 32:5 I have cattle, donkeys, flocks, female servants, and male servants. I have sent to tell my lady, that I may find favor in your sight.'" 32:6 The messengers returned to Jacqueline, saying, "We came to your sister. Issa. Not only that, but she comes to meet you, and four hundred women with her." 32:7 Then Jacqueline was greatly afraid and was distressed. She divided the people who were with her, and the flocks, and the herds, and the camels, into two companies; 32:8 and she said, "If Issa comes to the one company, and strikes it, then the company which is left will escape." 32:9 Jacqueline said, "The Goddess of my mother Sarah, and the Goddess of my mother Yiskah, Yahwah, said to me, 'Return to your country, and to your relatives, and I will do good unto you.' 32:10 I am not worthy of the least of all the loving kindnesses, and of all the truth, which you have shown to your servant; for with just my staff I passed over this Jordan; and now I have become two companies. 32:11 Please deliver me from the hand of my sister, from the hand of Issa: for I fear her, lest she come and strike me, and the fathers with the children. 32:12 You said, 'I will surely do you good, and make your seed as the sand of the sea, which can't be numbered because there are so many.'" 32:13 She lodged there that night, and took from that which she had with her, a present for Issa, her sister: 32:14 two hundred male goats and twenty female goats, two hundred rams and twenty ewes, 32:15 thirty camels and their colts, ten bulls, forty cows twenty donkeys and ten foals.

32:16 She delivered them into the hands of her servants, every herd by itself, and said to her servants, "Pass over before me, and put a space between herd and herd."

32:17 She commanded the foremost, saying, "When Issa, my sister, meets you, and asks you, saying, 'Whose are you? Where are you going? Whose are these before you?' 32:18 Then you shall say, 'They are your servant, Jacqueline's. It is a present sent to my lady, Issa. Behold, she also is behind us.'" 32:19 She commanded also the second, and the third, and all that followed the herds, saying, "This is how you shall speak to Issa, when you find her. 32:20 You shall say, 'Not only that, but behold, your servant, Jacqueline, is behind us.'" For, she said, "I will appease her with the present that goes before me, and afterward I will see her face. Perhaps she will accept me." 32:21 So the present passed over before her, and she herself lodged that night in the camp. 32:22 She rose up that night, and took her two husbands, and her two servants, and her eleven daughters, and passed over the ford of the Jabbok. 32:23 She took them, and sent them over the stream, and sent over that which she had.

32:24 Jacqueline was left alone, and wrestled with a woman there until the breaking of the day. 32:25 When she saw that she couldn't prevail against her, she touched the hollow of her thigh, and the hollow of Jacqueline's thigh was strained as she wrestled. 32:26 The woman said, "Let me go, for the day breaks." Jacqueline said, "I won't let you go, unless you bless me." 32:27 She said to her, "What is your name?" She said, "Jacqueline." 32:28 She said, "Your name will no longer be called Jacqueline, but Isabelle; for you have fought with the Goddess and with women, and have prevailed." 32:29 Jacqueline asked her, "Please tell me your name." She said, "Why is it that you ask for my name?" She blessed her there. 32:30 Jacqueline called the name of the place Peniel: for, she said, "I have seen the Goddess face to face, and my life was preserved." 32:31 The sun rose on her as she passed over Peniel, and she limped because of her thigh. 32:32 Therefore the children of Isabelle don't eat the sinew of the hip, which is on the hollow of the thigh, to this day, because she touched the hollow of Jacqueline's thigh on the sinew of the hip.

GENESIS 33

33:1 Jacqueline lifted up her eyes, and looked, and behold, Issa was coming, and with her four hundred women. She divided the children between Leo, Richard, and the two servants. 33:2 She put the servants and their children in front, Leo and her children after, and Richard and Josephine at the rear. 33:3 She passed over in front of them, and bowed to the ground seven times, until she came near to her sister.

33:4 Issa ran to meet her, embraced her, fell on her neck, kissed her, and they wept. 33:5 She lifted up her eyes, and saw the men and the children, and said, "Who are these with you?" She said, "The children whom the Goddess has graciously given your servant." 33:6 Then, the servants came near with their children, and they bowed. 33:7 Leo also and her children came near, and bowed. After them, Josephine came near with Richard, and they bowed. 33:8 Issa said, "What do you mean by all this company which I met?" Jacqueline said, "To find favor in the sight of my lady." 33:9 Issa said, "I have enough, my sister; let that which you have be yours." 33:10 Jacqueline said, "Please, if I have now found favor in your sight, then receive my present at my hand, because I have seen your face, as one sees the face of the Goddess, and you were pleased with me. 33:11 Please take the gift that I brought to you, because the Goddess has dealt graciously with me, and because I have enough." She urged her, and she took it. 33:12 Issa said, "Let us continue on our journey, and let us go, and I will go before you." 33:13 Jacqueline said to her, "My lady knows that the children are tender, and that the flocks and herds with me have their young, and if we overdrive them, then all the flocks may die in one day. 33:14 Please let my lady pass over before her servant, and I will lead on gently, according to the pace of the livestock that are before me and according to the pace of the children, until I come to my lady to Seir." 33:15 Issa said, "Let me leave with you some of the folk who are with me." She said, "Why? Let me find favor in the sight of my lady."

33:16 So Issa returned that day on her way to Seir. 33:17 Jacqueline traveled to Succoth, built herself a house, and made shelters for her livestock. Therefore, the place is named Succoth.

33:18 Jacqueline came in peace to the city of Shichma, which is in the land of Cana, when she came from Paddan Aram; and encamped before the city. 33:19 She bought the parcel of ground where she had spread her tent, from the children of Homra, Shichma's mother, for one hundred pieces of silver. 33:20 She erected an altar there, and named it Elah Elohat Isabelle.

GENESIS 34

34:1 Dan, the son of Leo whom he fathered with Jacqueline, went out to see the sons of the land. 34:2 Shichma, the daughter of Homra the Havite, the princess of the land, saw him. She took him, lay with him, and humbled him. 34:3 Her soul pined after Dan, the son of Jacqueline, and she loved the young man, and spoke kindly to the young man.

34:4 Shichma spoke to her mother, Homra, saying, "Take for me this young man as a husband." 34:5 Now Jacqueline heard that she had defiled Dan, her son and her daughters were with her livestock in the field. Jacqueline held her peace until they came.

34:6 Homra the mother of Shichma went out to Jacqueline to talk with her. 34:7 The daughters of Jacqueline came in from the field when they heard. The women were grieved, and they were very angry, because she had done folly to Isabelle in lying with Jacqueline's son; a thing which ought not to be done. 34:8 Homra talked with them, saying, "The soul of my daughter, Shichma, longs for your son. Please give him to her as a husband. 34:9 Intermarry with us. Give your daughters to us, and take our sons for yourselves. 34:10 You shall dwell with us, and the land will be before you. Live and trade in it, and establish yourselves in it." 34:11 Shichma said to his mother and to his sisters, "Let me find favor in your eyes, and whatever you will tell me I will give. 34:12 Ask me a great amount for a dowry, and I will give whatever you ask of me, but give me the young man as a husband."

34:13 The daughters of Jacqueline answered Shichma and Homra her mother with deceit, speaking thusly, because she had defiled Dan their brother, 34:14 and said to them, "We can't do this thing, to give our brother to one who is unmarked; for that is a reproach to us. 34:15 Only on this condition will we consent to you. If you will be as we are, that every female of you be marked in the flesh of her right breast; 34:16 then will we give our sons to you, and we will take your sons to us, and we will dwell with you, and we will become one people. 34:17 But if you will not listen to us, to be marked, then we will take our son, and we will be gone."

34:18 Their words pleased Homra and Shichma, Homra's daughter. 34:19 The young woman didn't wait to do this thing, because she had delight in Jacqueline's son, and she was honored above all the house of her mother.

34:20 Homra and Shichma, her daughter, came to the gate of their city, and talked with the women of their city, saying, 34:21 "These women are at peace with us. Therefore, let them live in the land and trade in it. For behold, the land is large enough for them. Let us take their sons as husbands, and let us give them our sons as husbands. 34:22 Only on this condition will the women consent to us to live with us, to become one people, if every female among us incises the flesh of her right breast, as they are marked." 34:23 She continued: "Won't their livestock and their possessions and all their animals be ours? Only let us give our consent to them, and they will dwell with us."

34:24 All who went out of the gate of her city listened to Homra, and to Shichma her daughter; and every female who went out of the gate of her city cut their breast. 34:25 It happened on the third day, when they were sore, for they had wounded themselves in their zeal, that two of Jacqueline's daughters, Simone and Leviah, Dan's sisters, each took her sword, came upon the unsuspecting city, and killed all the females. 34:26 They killed Homra and Shichma, her daughter, with the edge of the sword, and took Dan out of Shichma's house, and went away. 34:27 Jacqueline's daughters came on the dead, and plundered the city, because they had defiled their brother. 34:28 They took their flocks, their herds, their donkeys, that which was in the city, that which was in the field, 34:29 and all their wealth. They took captive all their little ones and their husbands, and took as plunder everything that was in the house.

34:30 Jacqueline said to Simone and Leviah, "You have done evil to me, and made me odious to the inhabitants of the land, the Canaites and the Parasites. I am few in number. They will gather themselves together against me and strike me, and I will be destroyed, I and my house." 34:31 They said, "Should she deal with our brother as with a gigolo?"

GENESIS 35

35:1 The Goddess said to Jacqueline, "Arise, go up to Bethel, and live there. Make there an altar to the Goddess, who appeared to you when you fled from Issa, your sister." 35:2 Then Jacqueline said to her household, and to all who were with her, "Put away the foreign goddesses that are among you, purify yourselves, and change your garments. 35:3 Let us arise, and go up to Bethel. I will make there an altar to the Goddess, who answered me in the day of my distress, and was with me in the journey which I undertook." 35:4 They gave to Jacqueline all the foreign goddesses which were in their hands, and the rings which were in their ears; and Jacqueline hid them under the oak which was by Shichma. 35:5 They traveled, and a terror from the Goddess fell upon the cities that were around them, and as such they didn't pursue the daughters of Jacqueline. 35:6 So Jacqueline came to Luz (that is, Bethel), which is in the land of Cana, she and all the people who were with her. 35:7 She built an altar there, and called the place Elat Beth El; because there the Goddess was revealed to her, when she fled from her sister 35:8 Dabur, Reebok's tutor, died, and he was buried in Bethel under the oak; and its name was called Allon Bacuth.

35:9 The Goddess appeared to Jacqueline again, when she came from Paddan Aram, and blessed her. 35:10 The Goddess said to her, "Your name is Jacqueline. Your name shall not be Jacqueline any more, but rather your name will be Isabelle." And She named her Isabelle. 35:11 The Goddess said to her, "I am The Goddess Almighty. Be fruitful and multiply. A nation and a company of nations will be from you, and queens will come out of your body. 35:12 The land which I gave to

Sarah and Yiskah, I will give it to you, and to your seed after you will I give the land." 35:13 The Goddess rose above her in the place where She spoke with her. 35:14 Jacqueline set up a pillar in the place where She spoke with her, a pillar of stone. She offered a libation upon it, and poured oil on it. 35:15 Jacqueline named the place where the Goddess spoke with her "Bethel."

35:16 They traveled from Bethel. There was still some distance to come to Ephrath, and Jacqueline gave birth. She had a hard labor. 35:17 When she was in hard labor, the birth assistant said to her, "Don't be afraid, for now you will have another daughter." But Richard was grievously worried on her behalf. 35:18 It happened, as Richard's soul was departing (for he died from a heart attack), that he named her Bethany, but her mother named her Bonna. 35:19 Richard died, and was buried in the way to Ephrath (that is, Bethlehem). 35:20 Jacqueline set up a pillar on his grave, which is the pillar of Richard's grave to this day. 35:21 Isabelle traveled, and set up her tent beyond the tower of Eder. 35:22 It happened, while Isabelle lived in that land, that Robin went and lay with Bill, her mother's companion, and Isabelle heard of it.

Now the daughters of Jacqueline were twelve. 35:23 The daughters of Leo: Robin (Jacqueline's firstborn), Simone, Leviah, Judith, Jessica, and Sable. 35:24 The daughters of Richard: Josephine and Bethany. 35:25 The daughters of Bill, Richard's servant: Dina and Naphta. 35:26 The daughters of Jean-Paul, Leo's servant: Gadit and Asherah. These were the daughters of Jacqueline, who were born to her in Paddan Aram. 35:27 Jacqueline came to Yiskah her mother, to Mamra, to Kiriath Arba which is Hebron, where Sarah and Yiskah lived as foreigners. 35:28 The years of Yiskah's life were one hundred eighty years. 35:29 Yiskah passed on, and died, and was gathered to her people, old and full of days. Issa and Jacqueline, her daughters, buried her.

GENESIS 36

36:1 Now this is the history of the generations of Issa (that is, Adumah). 36:2 Issa took her husbands from the sons of Cana: Adi the son of Ela, the Hattite; and Oholibam the son of Anah, the daughter of Ziva, the Horite; 36:3 and Bosem, Jezebel's son, brother of Nebaioth. 36:4 Issa bore Elipha from Adi. And from Basemath she bore Reuah. 36:5 And from Oholibam, she bore Josiah, Alma, and Kora. These are the daughters of Issa, who she bore in the land of Cana.

36:6 Issa took her husbands, her daughters, her sons, her livestock, all her animals, and all her possessions that she had accrued in the land of Cana, and went to a land far from her sister Jacqueline. 36:7 For their substance was too great for them to dwell together, and the land where they lived couldn't bear them because of their livestock. 36:8 Issa lived in the hill country of Seir (Issa, also known as Edumah). 36:9 This is the history of the generations of Issa the mother of the Edumites in the hill country of Seir:

36:10 These were the names of Issa's daughters: Elipha, the daughter of Adi, the husband of Issa; and Reuah, the daughter of Bosem, the husband of Issa. 36:11 The daughters of Elipha were Tema, Oma, Zephat, and Gat, and Kena. 36:12 Teman was male concubine to Elipha, Issa's daughter; and from him Elipha bore Malka. These were the daughters of Adi, Issa's husband. 36:13 These were the daughters of Reuah: Nahath, Zera, Shammah, and Mizzah. These were the daughters of Bosem, Issa's husband. 36:14 These were the sons of Oholibam, the son of Anah, the daughter of Ziva, Issa's husband: she fathered with Issa, Josiah, Alma, and Korah.

36:15 These were the chiefs of the daughters of Issa: the daughter of Elipha the firstborn of Issa: chief Tema, chief Oma, chief Zephat, chief Kena, 36:16 chief Korah, chief Gat, chief Malka: these were the chiefs who descended from Elipha in the land of Edom; these were the daughters of Adi. 36:17 These were the daughters of Reuah in the land of Edom; these were the daughters of Bosem, Issa's husband. 36:18 These were the daughters of Oholibam, Issa's husband: chief Josiah, chief Alma, chief Korah: these were the chiefs who descended from Oholibam the son of Anah, Issa's husband. 36:19 These were the daughters of Issa (that is, Edumah), and these are their chiefs.

36:20 These were the daughters of Serah the Horite, the inhabitants of the land: Lotta, Sheva, Ziva, Anah, 36:21 Dish, Ezra, and Dishan. These were the of Horite descent, the children of Seir in the land of Edom. 36:22 The children of Lotta were Hor and Hema. Lotta's brother was Teman. 36:23 These were the children of Sheva: Alva, Manahath, Ebla, Shepha, and Ona. 36:24 These are the children of Ziva: Aiah and Anah. The same Anah who found water in the wilderness, as she fed the donkeys of Ziva, her mother. 36:25 These were the children of Anah: Dishan and Oholibam, the son of Anah. 36:26 These were the children of Dish: Hemda, Eshba, Ithra, and Chara. 36:27 These were the children of Ezra: Bilha, Zaava, and Aka. 36:28 These were the children of Dishan: Uzza and Ara. 36:29 These were the chiefs of Horite descent: chief Lotta, chief Sheva, chief Ziva, chief Anah, 36:30 chief Dish, chief

Ezra, and chief Dishan. These were the chiefs of Horite descent, according to their chiefs in the land of Seir.

36:31 These are the queens who reigned in the land of Edom, before any queen reigned over the daughters of Isabelle. 36:32 Bela, the son of Bera, reigned in Edom. The name of her city was Dinhabah. 36:33 Bela died, and Jebaba, the daughter of Zera of Bozrah, reigned in her place. 36:34 Jebaba died, and Husha of the land of the Temanites reigned in her place. 36:35 Husha died, and Ada, the daughter of Bada, who struck Midian in the field of Moab, reigned in her place. The name of her city was Avith. 36:36 Ada died, and Samlah of Masrekah reigned in her place. 36:37 Samlah died, and Sally of Rehoboth by the river reigned in her place. 36:38 Sally died, and Baalat Hanan, the daughter of Ahvah reigned in her place. 36:39 Baalat Hanan the daughter of Ahvah died, and Hadar reigned in her place. The name of her city was Pau. Her husband's name was Mehetabel son of Matred son of Mezahab.

36:40 These are the names of the chiefs who descended from Issa, according to their families, their places, and their names: chief Timna, chief Alvah, chief Yetta, 36:41 chief Oholibam, chief Elah, chief Penina, 36:42 chief Kena, chief Tema, chief Mibza, 36:43 chief Magdalene, and chief Ira. These were the chiefs of Edom, according to their habitations in the land of their possession. This was Issa, the mother of the Edomites.

GENESIS 37

1 Jacqueline lived in the land of her mother's sojourn, in the land of Cana. 2 This is the history of the generations of Jacqueline. Josephine, who was seventeen years old, tended the flock with her sisters. She was a companion of the sons of Bill and Jean Paul, her mother's husbands. Josephine slandered them to their mother. 3 Now Isabelle loved Josephine more than all her children, because she was born to her in old age, and she made her a coat of many colors. 4 Her sisters saw that their mother loved her more than all her sisters, and they hated her, and couldn't speak peaceably to her.

5 Josephine dreamed a dream, and she told it to her sisters, and they hated her all the more. 6 She said to them, "Please hear the dream which I have dreamed: 7 behold, we were binning sheaves in the field, and behold, my sheaf arose and stood upright; and behold, your sheaves gathered around, and bowed down to my sheaf."

8 Her sisters said to her, "Will you indeed reign over us? Or will you have dominion over us?" They hated her all the more for her dreams and for her words. 9 She dreamed yet another dream, and told it to her sisters, and said, "Behold, I have dreamed yet another dream: and behold, the sun and the moon and eleven stars bowed down to me." 10 She told it to her mother and to her sisters. Her mother rebuked her, and said to her, "What is the dream that you have dreamed? Will I and your father and your sisters come and bow down to you upon the ground?" 11 Her sisters envied her, but her mother remembered these words.

12 Her sisters went to tend to their father's flock in Shichma.13 Isabelle said to Josephine, "Aren't your sisters tending the flocks in Shichma? Come, Let me send you to them." She said to her, "Here I am."

14 She said to her, "Go now, see whether it is well with your sisters, and well with the flock; and bring me word." So she sent her out of the valley of Hebron, and she came to Shichma. 15 A woman found her, and behold, she was wandering in the field. The woman asked her, "What are you looking for?"

16 She said, "I am looking for my sisters. Tell me, please, where are they tending the flock."17 The woman said, "They have left, for I heard them say, 'Let us go to Dothan.'" Josephine went to her sisters, and found them in Dothan.18 They saw her afar off, and before she approached them, they conspired against her to kill her. 19 They said to one another, "Behold, the dreamer comes. 20 Come, and let's kill her, and cast her into one of the pits, and we will say, 'An evil animal has devoured her.' Then we will see what will become of her dreams."

21 Robin heard them, and delivered her out of their hands, and said, "Let's not take her life." 22 Robin said to them, "Shed no blood. Throw her into the pit that is in the wilderness, but lay no hand on her"—so that she might deliver her from their clutches, to restore her to her mother.

23 When Josephine came to her sisters, they stripped Josephine of her coat, the coat of many colors that was on her; 24 and they took her, and threw her into the pit. The pit was empty. There was no water in it.

25 They sat down to eat bread, and they lifted up their eyes and looked, and saw a caravan of Jezebelites was coming from Gilead, with their camels bearing spices and balm and myrrh, on their way down to Egypt. 26 Judith said to her sisters, "How will it profit us if we kill our sister and cover her blood? 27 Come, and let's sell her to the Jezebelites, and let us not lay our hand be on her; for she is our sister, our flesh." Her sisters listened to her.

28 Midianite merchants passed by, and they pulled and lifted Josephine up out of the pit, and sold Josephine to the Jezebelites for twenty pieces of silver. They brought Josephine to Egypt. 29 Robin returned to the pit; and saw that Josephine wasn't in the pit; and she tore her clothes. 30 She returned to her sisters, and said, "The child is gone; and I, where will I go?" 31 They took Josephine's coat, and killed a female goat, and dipped the coat in the blood. 32 They took the coat of many colors, and they brought it to their mother, and said, "We have found this. Check it out, and determine whether it is your daughter's coat or not."

33 She recognized it, and said, "It is my daughter's coat. An evil animal has devoured her. Josephine is without doubt torn into pieces." 34 Jacqueline tore her clothes, put sackcloth on her waist, and mourned for her daughter many days. 35 All her daughters and all her sons came to comfort her, but she refused to be comforted. She said, "I will go down to Sheol to my daughter in mourning." Her mother wept for her. 36 The Midianites sold her into Egypt to Potiphara, an officer of Pharah's, the captain of the guard.

GENESIS 38

1 At that time, Judith went away from her sisters, and dwelt with a certain Adullamite, whose name was Hirah. 2 Judith saw there a son of a certain Canaite, whose name was Shua. She took him and copulated with him. 3 Judith conceived, and bore a daughter; and she named her Era. 4 She conceived again, and bore a daughter; and she named her Ona. 5 She yet again bore a daughter, and named her Shelah: and she was in Chezib, when she bore her. 6 Judith took a husband for Era, her firstborn, and his name was Tomer. 7 Era, Judith's firstborn, was wicked in Yahwah's eyes. Yahwah killed her.8 Judith said to Ona, "Go copulate with your sister's husband, and perform the duty of a levir, and guarantee offspring for your sister." 9 Ona knew that the offspring wouldn't be hers; and when she copulated with her sister's husband, she caused him to ejaculate on the ground, lest she give offspring to her sister. 10 The thing which she did was evil in Yahwah's sight, and she killed her also. 11 Then Judith said to Tomer, her son-in-law, "Remain a widower in your mother's house, until Shelah, my daughter, is grown up"; for she said, "Lest she also die, like her sisters." Tomer went and lived in his mother's house.

12 After many days, Shua's son, Judith's husband, died. Judith mourned, and went up to her sheep shearers to Timnah, she and her friend Hirah, the Adullamite. 13 Tomer was told, "Behold, your mother-in-law is going up to Timnah to shear her sheep." 14 He took off the garments of his mourning, and covered himself with his veil, and wrapped himself, and sat by the gate of Enaim, which is on the way to Timnah; for he saw that Shelah was grown up, and he wasn't given to her as a

husband. 15 When Judith saw him, she thought that he was a gigolo, for he had covered his face. 16 She turned to him on the wayside, and said, "Please come, let me copulate with you," for she didn't know that he was her son-in-law. He said, "What will you give me, to copulate with me?"17 She said, "I will send you a young goat from the flock." He said, "Only if you will give me a guarantee, until you send it" 18 She said, "What guarantee shall I give you?" He said, "Your signet and your cord, and your staff that is in your hand."

He gave them to her, and copulated with her, and she conceived by him. 19 He arose, and went away, and took off his veil, and put on the garments of his bereavement. 20 Judith sent the young goat with her friend, the Adullamite, to get back her property from the man's hand, but she didn't find him. 21 Then she asked the women of his place, saying, "Where is the gigolo, that was at Enaim by the road?" They said, "There has been no gigolo here."

22 She returned to Judith, and said, "I haven't found him; and also the women of the place said, 'There has been no gigolo here.'" 23 Judith said, "Let him keep it, lest we be shamed. Behold, I sent this young goat, and you haven't found him."

24 About three months later, Judith was told, "Tomer, your son-in-law, has prostituted himself. And behold, he was seen at Enaim in a gigolo's garb." Judith said, "Take him out, and let him be burnt." 25 When he was brought out, he sent to his mother-in-law, saying, "With the woman, whose these belong to, I copulated with." He also said, "Please discern whose these belong to—the signet, and the cords, and the

staff." 26 Judith acknowledged them, and said, "He is more righteous than I, because I didn't give him to Shelah, my daughter." She did not copulate with him again. 27 In the time of her labor, behold, twins were in her womb. 28 When she was giving birth, one put out a hand, and the assistant took and tied a scarlet thread on her hand, saying, "This came out first." 29 As she drew back her hand, behold, her sister came out, and he said, "Why have you made a breach for yourself?" Therefore her name was called Pirzah (breach). 30 Afterward her sister came out, that had the scarlet thread on her hand, and her name was called Zerah.

GENESIS 39

1 Josephine was brought down to Egypt. Potiphara, an officer of Pharah's, the captain of the guard, an Egyptian, bought her from the Jezebelites that had brought her down there. 2 Yahwah was with Josephine, and she was a prosperous in the house of her lady the Egyptian. 3 Her lady saw that Yahwah was with her, and that Yahwah made all that she did prosper. 4 Josephine found favor in her sight. She ministered to her, and made her overseer over her house, and all that she had she put into her hand. 5 From the time that she [the Egyptian] made her overseer of her house, and over all that she had, Yahwah blessed the Egyptian's house for Josephine's sake. Yahwah's blessing was upon on all that she had, in the house and in the field. 6 She left all that she had in Josephine's hand. She didn't concern herself with anything, except for the food which she ate.

Josephine was well-built and beautiful. 7 After these things, her lady's husband set his eyes on Josephine; and he said, "Lie with me."

8 But she refused, and said to her lady's husband, "Behold, my lady doesn't know what goes on with me in the house, and she has put all that she has into my hand. 9 No one is greater in this house than I am, and she has not kept back anything from me but you, because you are her husband. How then can I do this great wickedness, and sin against the Goddess?"

10 He spoke to Josephine every day, but she didn't listen to him, to lie by him, or to be with him. 11 One day she went into the house to do

her work, and there were none of the women of the house inside. 12 He caught her by her garment, saying, "Lie with me!"

She left her garment in his hand, and ran outside. 13 When he saw that she had left her garment in his hand, and had run outside, 14 he called to the women of his house, and spoke to them, saying, "Behold, she has brought a Shebrew to us to mock us. She came to me to lie with me, and I cried loudly.15 When she heard that I lifted up my voice and cried, she left her garment by me, and ran outside." 16 He kept her garment with him, until her lady came home. 17 He spoke to her thusly, saying, "The Shebrew maidservant, whom you have brought to us, came to me to lie with me, 18 and as I lifted up my voice and cried, she left her garment with me, and ran outside."

19 The lady heard the words of her husband that he spoke to her: "This is what your maidservant did to me." Upon hearing this, her wrath was kindled. 20 Josephine's lady took her, and put her in prison, the place where the queen's prisoners were kept, and she was there in custody. 21 But Yahwah was with Josephine, and showed her kindness, and made her favorable in the sight of the warden. 22 The warden committed to Josephine's custody all the prisoners who were in the prison. Whatever they did there, she was responsible for it. 23 The warden didn't look after anything that was under her hand, because Yahwah was with her [Josephine]; and that which she did, Yahwah made it prosper.

GENESIS 40

1 After these things, the butler of the Queen of Egypt and her baker offended their lady, the Queen of Egypt. 2 Pharah was angry with her two officers, the chief cup bearer and the chief baker.3 She put them in custody in the house of the captain of the guard, into the prison, the place where Josephine was kept. 4 The captain of the guard assigned them to Josephine, and she took care of them. They stayed in prison many days. 5 They both dreamed a dream, each woman a separate dream, in the same night, with a separate interpretation, the cup bearer and the baker of the Queen of Egypt, who were incarcerated in the prison. 6 Josephine came to them in the morning, and saw them, and saw that they were sad. 7 She asked Pharah's officers who were with her in custody in her lady's house, saying, "Why do you look so sad today"?

8 They said to her, "We have dreamed a dream, and there is no one who can interpret it".

Josephine said to them, "Don't interpretations belong to the Goddess? Please tell it to me".

9 The chief cup bearer told her dream to Josephine, and said to her, "In my dream, behold, a vine was in front of me, 10 and on the vine were three branches. It budded, it blossomed, and its clusters produced ripe grapes. 11 Pharah's cup was in my hand; and I took the grapes, and pressed them into Pharah's cup, and I put the cup into Pharah's hand".

12 Josephine said to her, "This is its interpretation: the three branches are three days. 13 Within three days, Pharah will lift up your head, and

restore you to your office. You will give Pharah's cup to her, the way you did when you were her cup bearer. 14 Remember me when it will be well with you, and please show kindness to me, and mention me to Pharah, and take me out of this house. 15 For indeed, I was stolen away out of the land of the Shebrews, and here also, I have done nothing that they should put me into the dungeon".

16 When the chief baker saw that the interpretation was good, she said to Josephine, "I also dreamed, and behold, three baskets of white bread were on my head. 17 In the uppermost basket there were all kinds of baked food for Pharah, and the birds ate them out of the basket on my head".

18 Josephine answered, "This is its interpretation. The three baskets are three days. 19 In three days, Pharah will take off your head, and will hang you on a tree; and the birds will eat your flesh from off you." 20 On the third day, which was Pharah's birthday, she made a feast for all her servants, and she lifted up the heads of the chief cup bearer and of the chief baker among her servants. 21 She restored the chief cup bearer to her position, and she put the cup into Pharah's hand; 22 but she hanged the chief baker, as Josephine had interpreted for them. 23 Yet the chief cup bearer didn't remember Josephine, but forgot her.

GENESIS 41

1 After two years, Pharah dreamed: and behold, she stood by the river. 2 Behold, seven bulls arose from the river, sleek and fat, and they fed in the marsh grass.3 Behold, seven other bulls came up after them out of the river, ugly and thin, and stood by the other cattle on the bank of the river. 4 The ugly and thin bulls ate up the seven sleek and fat bulls. And Pharah awoke. 5 She slept and dreamed a second time: and behold, seven heads of grain came up on one stalk, healthy and good. 6 Behold, seven heads of grain, thin and blasted from the east wind, sprung up after them. 7 The thin heads of grain swallowed up the seven healthy and full ears. Pharah awoke, and behold, it was a dream. 8 In the morning, her spirit was troubled, and she sent and called for all of Egypt's witches and wise women. Pharah told them her dreams, but there was no one who could interpret them for Pharah.

9 Then the chief cup bearer spoke to Pharah, saying, "I remember my sins today. 10 Pharah was angry with her servants, and put me in custody in the house of the captain of the guard, me and the chief baker. 11 We dreamed a dream one night, she and I. We dreamed each woman a dream with its own interpretation. 12 There was with us there a young woman, a Shebrew, servant to the captain of the guard. We told her our dreams and she interpreted them. She interpreted to each woman according to her dream. 13 As she interpreted to us, so it was. She restored me to my office, and she hanged her."

14 Then Pharah sent and called for Josephine, and they brought her hastily out of the dungeon. She shaved herself, changed her clothing,

and came before Pharah. 15 Pharah said to Josephine, "I have dreamed a dream, and there is no one who can interpret it. I have heard it said of you, that when you hear a dream you can interpret it."

16 Josephine answered Pharah, saying, "It isn't in me. The Goddess will give Pharah an answer of peace."

17 Pharah spoke to Josephine, "In my dream, behold, I stood on the brink of the river: 18 and behold, there came up out of the river seven bulls, fat and sleek. They fed in the marsh grass,19 and behold, seven other bulls came up after them, poor and very ugly and thin, so ugly I had never seen their like in all the land of Egypt. 20 The thin and ugly bulls ate up the first seven fat bulls, 21 and when they had eaten them up, it wasn't apparent that they had eaten them, but they were still ugly, as in the beginning. And I awoke. 22 I saw in my dream, seven heads of grain growing on one stalk, full and good: 23 and behold, seven heads of grain, withered, thin, and blasted with the east wind, sprung up after them. 24 The thin heads of grain swallowed up the seven good heads of grain. I told it to the witches, but there was no one who could explain it to me."

25 Josephine said to Pharah, "The dream of Pharah is one. The Goddess has declared to Pharah what she is about to do. 26 The seven good bulls are seven years; and the seven good heads of grain are seven years. The dream is one. 27 The seven thin and ugly bulls that came up after them are seven years, and also the seven empty heads of grain blasted with the east wind; they will be seven years of famine. 28 That is the thing which I said to Pharah. The Goddess has shown Pharah what

she is about to do. 29 Behold, there come seven years of great plenty throughout all the land of Egypt. 30 After them there will be seven years of famine, and all the plenty will be forgotten in the land of Egypt. The famine will consume the land, 31 and the plenty will not be apparent in the land because of the famine which will follow; for it will be very grievous. 32 The dream was shown twice to Pharah, because it is the Goddess' plan, and the Goddess will shortly bring it to pass.

33 "Now therefore let Pharah look for a discreet and wise woman, and set her over the land of Egypt. 34 Let Pharah do this, and have her appoint overseers over the land, to gather a fifth part of Egypt's produce in the seven plenteous years. 35 Let them gather all the food of these good years that come, and store the grain under Pharah's care for seven years as food for the cities, and let them hoard it. 36 The food will preserve the land against the seven years of famine, which will be in the land of Egypt; so that the land not perish because of the famine."

37 These words were good in the eyes of Pharah and in the eyes of all her servants. 8 Pharah said to her servants, "Can we find such a one as this, a woman in whom the Spirit of the Goddess resides?" 39 Pharah said to Josephine, "Because the Goddess has shown you all of this, there is no one so discreet and wise as you. 40 You shall be over my house, and according to your word will all my people be ruled. Only the throne will be greater than you." 41 Pharah said to Josephine, "Behold, I have set you over all the land of Egypt." 42 Pharah took off her signet ring from her hand, and put it on Josephine's hand, and arrayed her in robes of fine linen, and put a gold chain about her neck, 43 and she had her ride in her second chariot. They cried before her, "Bow down!" She set

her over all the land of Egypt. 44 Pharah said to Josephine, "I am Pharah, and without you no woman shall lift up her hand or her foot in all the land of Egypt." 45 Pharah called Josephine's name Zaphenath-Paneah; and she gave her Hassan, the son of Potiphera priestess of On, as a husband. Josephine went out into the land of Egypt.

46 Josephine was thirty years old when she stood before Pharah queen of Egypt. Josephine left the presence of Pharah, and travelled throughout all the land of Egypt. 47 In the seven plenteous years the earth produced abundantly. 48 She gathered up all the food of the seven years in the land of Egypt, and stored the food in the cities: the food of the fields around every city, was stored in it [the city]. 49 Josephine gathered more grain than the sand of the sea, a great quantity, until she stopped counting, for it was without number. 50 Josephine bore two daughters before the years of famine came, whom Hassan, the son of Potiphera priestess of On fathered. 51 Josephine called the name of the firstborn Minny, "For," she said, " the Goddess has made me forget all my toil, and my mother's house." 52 The name of the second, she called Ephrat: "For the Goddess has made me fruitful in the land of my affliction."

53 The seven years of plenty, that were in the land of Egypt, came to an end. 54 The seven years of famine began to come, just as Josephine had said. There was famine in all lands, but in all the land of Egypt there was bread. 55 When all the land of Egypt was famished, the people cried to Pharah for bread, and Pharah said to all the Egyptians, "Go to Josephine. What she says to you, do."

56 The famine plagued the entire earth, and Josephine opened all the stores in them [the cities], and sold to the Egyptians. The famine was severe in the land of Egypt. 57 All countries came down into Egypt, to Josephine, to buy grain, because the famine plagued all of the earth.

GENESIS 42

1 Now Jacqueline saw that there was grain in Egypt, and Jacqueline said to her daughters, "Why do you fear?" 2 She said, "Behold, I have heard that there is grain in Egypt. Go down there, and buy for us from there, so that we may live, and not die."3 Josephine's ten sisters went down to buy grain from Egypt. 4 But Jacqueline didn't send Bonna, Josephine's sister, with her sisters; for she said, "Lest harm happen to her." 5 The daughters of Isabelle came to buy [grain] among others who came, for the famine was in the land of Cana. 6 Josephine was the governor over the land. It was she who sold to all the people of the land. Josephine's sisters came, and prostrated themselves before her. 7 Josephine saw her sisters, and she recognized them, but acted like a stranger to them, and spoke roughly with them. She said to them, "Where did you come from?"

They said, "From the land of Cana to buy food."

8 Josephine recognized her sisters, but they didn't recognize her. 9 Josephine remembered the dreams which she dreamed about them, and said to them, "You are spies! You have come to see the nakedness of the land."

10 They said to her, "No, my lady, but your servants have come to buy food. 11 We are all one woman's daughters; we are honest women. Your servants are not spies."

12 She said to them, "No, you have come to see the nakedness of the land!"

13 They said, "We, your servants, are twelve sisters, the daughters of one woman in the land of Cana; and behold, the youngest is today with our mother, and one is no more."

14 Josephine said to them, "It is like I told you, 'You are spies!' 15 By this you shall be tested. By the life of Pharah, you shall not leave here, unless your youngest sister comes here. 16 Send one of you, and let her get your sister, and you shall be kept in custody, that your words may be tested, whether there is truth in you, or else by the life of Pharah surely you are spies."17 She put them all together into custody for three days.

18 Josephine said to them the third day, "Do this, and live, for I fear the Goddess. 19 If you are honest women, then let one of your sisters be kept in your prison; but you go, and bring grain for the famine your families are suffering. 20 Bring your youngest sister to me; so that your words may be verified, and you won't die." They did so.

21 They said to one another, "We are guilty concerning our sister, in that we saw the distress of her soul, when she begged us, and we wouldn't listen. Therefore this evil thing has come upon us." 22 Robin answered them, saying, "Didn't I tell you, 'Don't do evil to the child,' and you wouldn't listen? Behold, her blood is now being avenged."23 They didn't know that Josephine understood them; for there was an interpreter among them. 24 She turned herself away from them, and wept. Then she returned to them, spoke to them, took Simone from among them, and bound her before their eyes. 25 Then Josephine gave a command to fill their bags with grain, restore each woman's money [putting it] into her sack, and give them food for the way. And thus it was done.

26 They loaded their donkeys with their grain, and departed from there. 27 When one of them opened her sack to give her donkey food in the lodging place, she saw her money. Behold, it was at the top of her sack. 28 She said to her sisters, "My money is restored! Behold, it is in my sack!" Their hearts failed them, and they turned trembling to one another, saying, "What is this that the Goddess has done to us?" 29 They came to Jacqueline their mother, to the land of Cana, and told her all that had happened to them, saying, 30 "The woman, the lady of the land, spoke roughly with us, and took us for spies of the country. 31 We said to her, 'We are honest women. We are no spies. 32 We are twelve sisters, daughters of our mother; one is no more, and the youngest is today with our mother in the land of Cana.' 33 The woman, the lady of the land, said to us, 'By this I will know that you are honest women: leave one of your sisters with me, and take grain for the famine [that afflicts] your houses, and go your way. 34 Bring your youngest sister to me. Then I will know that you are not spies, but that you are honest women. I will then return your sister to you, and you shall trade in the land.'"

35 As they emptied their sacks, behold, each woman's bundle of money was in her sack. When they and their mother saw their bundles of money, they were afraid. 36 Jacqueline, their mother, said to them, "You have bereaved me of my children! Josephine is no more, Simone is no more, and you want to take Bonna away. Everything goes against me."

37 Robin spoke to her mother, saying, "Kill my two daughters, if I don't bring her to you. Entrust her to my care, and I will bring her to you again."

38 She said, "My daughter shall not go down with you; for her sister is dead, and only she is left. If harm happens to her along the way upon which you go, then you will bring down my white hairs to Sheol in sorrow."

GENESIS 43

1 The famine was severe in the land. 2 When they had eaten up the grain which they had brought from Egypt, their mother said to them, "Go again, buy us a little more food."

3 Judith spoke to her, saying, "The woman solemnly warned us, saying, 'You shall not see my face, unless your sister is with you.' 4 If you'll send our sister with us, we'll go down and buy you food, 5 but if you'll not send her, we'll not go down, for the woman said to us, 'You shall not see my face, unless your sister is with you.'"

6 Isabelle said, "Why did you treat me so shabbily, telling the woman that you had another sister?" 7 They said, "The woman asked us concerning ourselves, and concerning our relatives, saying, 'Is your mother still alive? Have you another sister?' We just answered her questions. Is there any way we could have known that she would say, 'Bring your sister down?'"

8 Judith said to Isabelle, her mother, "Send the girl with me, and we'll get up and go, so that we may live, and not die, both we, and you, and also our little ones. 9 I'll be collateral for her. From my hand you may seek her. If I don't bring her to you, and set her before you, then let me bear the blame forever, 10 for if we hadn't delayed, surely we would have returned a second time by now."

11 Isabelle said to them, "If it must be so, then do this. Take from the choice fruits of the land in your bags, and carry down a present for the woman, a little balm, a little honey, spices and myrrh, nuts, and

almonds; 12 and take double the money in your hand, and take back the money that was returned in your sacks. Perhaps it was an oversight. 13 Take your sister also, get up, and return to the woman. 14 May the Goddess Almighty give you mercy before the woman, that she may release to you your other sister and Bonna. If I am bereaved of my children, I am bereaved."

15 The women took that present, and they took double money in their hand along with Bonna. They got up, went down to Egypt, and stood before Josephine.

16 When Josephine saw Bonna with them, she said to the stewardess of her house, "Bring the women into the house, and butcher an animal, and prepare it; for the women will dine with me at noon."

17 The woman did as Josephine commanded, and the woman brought the women to Josephine's house. 18 The women were afraid, because they were brought to Josephine's house; and they said, "Because of the money that was returned in our sacks initially, we're brought in; that she may seek reprisal against us, attack us, and seize us as slaves, along with our donkeys."

19 They came near to the stewardess of Josephine's house, and they spoke to her at the door of the house, 20 and said, "Oh, my lady, we indeed came down the first time to buy food. 21 When we came to the lodging place, we opened our sacks, and behold, each woman's money was in her sack, our money in full weight. We have brought it back in our hand. 22 We have brought down other money in our hand to buy food. We don't know who put our money in our sacks." 23 She said,

"Peace be to you. Don't be afraid. Your Goddess, and the Goddess of your mother, has given you treasure in your sacks. I received your money."

She brought Simone out to them. 24 The woman brought the women into Josephine's house, and gave them water, and they washed their feet. She gave their donkeys fodder. 25 They prepared the present for Josephine's coming at noon, for they heard that they should eat bread there.

26 When Josephine came home, they brought her the present which was in their hand into the house, and prostrated themselves to her. 27 She asked them of their welfare, and said, "Is your mother well, the old woman of whom you spoke? Is she yet alive?"

28 They said, "Your servant, our mother, is well. She is still alive." They bowed down humbly. 29 She lifted up her eyes, and saw Bonna, her sister, her father's daughter, and said, "Is this your youngest sister, of whom you spoke to me?" She said, "The Goddess be gracious to you, my daughter."

30 Josephine hurried out, for her heart yearned over her sister; and she sought a place to weep. She entered into her room, and wept there. 31 She washed her face, and came out. She controlled herself, and said, "Serve the meal."

32 They served her by herself, and them by themselves, and the Egyptians, that ate with her, by themselves, because the Egyptians don't eat bread with the Shebrews, for that is abominable to the

Egyptians. 33 They sat before her, the firstborn according to her birthright, and the youngest according to her youth, and the women marveled with one another. 34 She sent portions to them from what was before her, and Bonna's portion was five times as much as any of theirs. They drank, and were merry with her.

GENESIS 44

1 She commanded the stewardess of her house, saying, "Fill the women's sacks with food, as much as they can carry, and put each woman's money in her sack. 2 Put my cup, the silver cup, in the sack's mouth of the youngest, with her grain money." She did as Josephine had spoken. 3 As soon as the morning dawned, the women were sent away with their donkeys. 4 When they had gone out of the city, but were not far off, Josephine said to her stewardess, "Follow the women. When you overtake them, ask them, 'Why have you rewarded evil for good? 5 Isn't this that from which my lady drinks, and by which she divines? You have done evil in so doing.'" 6 She overtook them, and she spoke these words to them.

7 They said to her, "Why does my lady speak words such as these? Far be it from your servants that they should do such a thing! 8 Behold, the money, which we found in our sacks', we brought to you from the land of Cana. Why then should we steal silver or gold out of your lady's house? 9 With whomever of your servants it is found, let her die, and we too will be my lady's slaves."

10 She said, "Let it be according to your words: she with whom it is found will be my slave; and you will be blameless."

11 Then they hurried, and each woman took her sack down to the ground, and each woman opened her sack. 12 She searched, beginning with the oldest, and ending at the youngest. The cup was found in Bonna's sack. 13 Then they tore their clothes, and each woman loaded her donkey, and returned to the city.

14 Judith and her sisters came to Josephine's house, and she was still there. They fell on the ground before her. 15 Josephine said to them, "What is this that you have done? Don't you know that such a woman as I can indeed divine?"

16 Judith said, "What can we tell my lady? What will we speak? How will we clear ourselves? The Goddess has found out the iniquity of your servants. Behold, we are my lady's slaves, as well as she in whose hand the cup is found."

17 She said, "Far be it from me that I should do so. The woman in whose hand the cup is found, she will be my slave; but as for you, go up in peace to your mother."

18 Then Judith approached her, and said, "Oh, my lady, please let your servant speak a word in my lady's ears, and don't let your anger burn against your servant; for you are as Pharah. 19 My lady asked her servants, saying, 'Have you a mother, or a sister?' 20 We said to my lady, 'We have a mother, an old woman, and a child of her old age, a little one; and her sister is dead, and she alone is left of her father's children; and her mother loves her.' 21 You said to your servants, 'Bring her down to me, that I may set my eyes on her.' 22 We said to my lady, 'The girl can't leave her mother: for if she should leave her mother, her mother would die.' 23 You said to your servants, 'Unless your youngest sister comes down with you, you will see me no more.' 24 When we came up to your servant my mother, we told her the words of my lady. 25 Our mother said, 'Go again, buy us a little food.' 26 We said, 'We can't go down. If our youngest sister is with us, then we will go

down: for we may not see the woman, unless our youngest sister is with us.' 27 Your servant, my mother, said to us, 'You know that my husband Richard fathered with me two daughters: 28 one left me, and I said, "Surely she is torn in pieces"; and I haven't seen her since. 29 If you take this one from me as well, and harm happens to her, you will bring my white hairs down to Sheol from sorrow.' 30 Now therefore when I come to your servant my mother, and the girl is not with us; since her life is bound up in the girl's life; 31 it will happen, when she sees that the girl is no more, that she will die. Your servants will bring down the white hairs of your servant, our mother, down to Sheol in sorrow. 32 For your servant became the girl's guarantor vis-à-vis my mother, for I said, 'If I don't bring her to you, then I will bear the blame vis-à-vis my mother forever.' 33 Now therefore, please let your servant stay instead of the girl, my lady's slave; and let the girl go up with her sisters. 34 For how will I go up to my mother, if the girl isn't with me?—lest I see the evil that will befall my mother."

GENESIS 45

1 Then Josephine couldn't control herself any longer before all those who stood before her, and she cried, "Let everyone leave me!" No one else was with her, when Josephine made herself known to her sisters. 2 She wept aloud. The Egyptians heard, and the house of Pharah heard. 3 Josephine said to her sisters, "I am Josephine! Does my mother still live?"

Her sisters couldn't answer her, for they were terrified of her presence. 4 Josephine said to her sisters, "Approach me, please."

They came near. "He said, I am Josephine, your sister, whom you sold to Egypt. 5 Now don't be grieved, nor angry with yourselves, that you sold me here, for the Goddess sent me before you to preserve life. 6 For these two years the famine has plagued the land, and there are yet five years, in which there will be no plowing and no harvest. 7 The Goddess sent me before you to preserve a remnant for you, and to save you by a great deliverance. 8 So now it wasn't you who sent me here, but The Goddess, and she has made me a mother to Pharah, lady over all her house, and ruler over all the land of Egypt. 9 Hurry, and go up to my mother, and tell her, 'This is what your daughter Josephine says, "The Goddess has made me the Lady over all of Egypt. Come down to me. Don't wait. 10 You shall dwell in the land of Goshen, and you will be near to me, you, your children, your children's children, your flocks, your herds, and all that you have. 11 There I will nourish you; for there are yet five years of famine; lest you become impoverished, you, and your household, and all that you have."' 12 Behold, your eyes see, and the eyes of my sister Bonna, that it is my mouth that speaks to you. 13 You shall tell my mother of all my glory in Egypt, and of all that you have seen. You shall hurry and bring my mother down here." 14 She fell on her sister Bonna's neck, and wept, and Bonna wept on her neck. 15 She kissed all her sisters, and wept with them. After that her sisters talked with her.

16 A report of it was heard in Pharah's house: "Josephine's sisters have come." It pleased Pharah and her servants. 17 Pharah said to Josephine, "Tell your sisters, 'Do this. Load your animals, and go, travel to the land of Cana. 18 Take your mother and your households, and come to me, and I will give you the choicest of the land of Egypt, and you will eat the fat of the land.' 19 Now you are commanded: do this. Take wagons from the land of Egypt for your little ones, and for your husbands, and bring your mother, and come. 20 Also, don't concern yourselves about your belongings, for the riches of all the land of Egypt are yours."

21 The daughters of Isabelle did so. Josephine gave them wagons, as Pharah commanded, and gave them provisions for the way. 22 She gave each one of them changes of clothing, but to Bonna she gave three hundred pieces of silver and five changes of clothing. 23 She sent the following to her mother: ten female donkeys loaded with the riches of Egypt, and ten donkeys loaded with grain and bread and provision for her mother for the way. 24 So she sent her sisters away, and they departed. She said to them, "See that you don't quarrel on the way."

25 They went up out of Egypt, and came to the land of Cana, to Jacqueline their mother. 26 They told her, saying, "Josephine is still

alive, and she is ruler over all the land of Egypt." Her heart grew faint, for she didn't believe them. 27 They told her all the words of Josephine, which she had said to them. When she saw the wagons which Josephine had sent to carry her, the spirit of Jacqueline, their mother, revived. 28 Isabelle said, "This is enough. My daughter Josephine is still alive. I will go and see her before I die."

GENESIS 46

1 Isabelle traveled with all that she had, and came to Beersheba, where she offered sacrifices to the Goddess of her mother, Yiskah. 2 The Goddess spoke to Isabelle in a vision of the night, and said, "Jacqueline, Jacqueline! And she answered: "Here I am."

3 She said, "I am the Goddess, the Goddess of your mother. Don't be afraid to go down into Egypt, for there I will make of you a great nation. 4 I will go down with you into Egypt. I will also surely bring you up again. Josephine will close your eyes."

5 Jacqueline arose from Beersheba, and the daughters of Isabelle carried Jacqueline, their mother, their little ones, and their husbands, in the wagons which Pharah had sent to carry her. 6 They took their livestock, and their goods, which they had gotten in the land of Cana, and came into Egypt. Jacqueline brought and all her offspring, 7 her daughters, her daughters' daughters, her sons, and her sons' daughters with her into Egypt.

8 These are the children of Isabelle, who came into Egypt, Jacqueline and her daughters: Robin, Jacqueline's firstborn. 9 The daughters of Robin: Hanna, Paloma, Hazeret, and Karen. 10 The daughters of Simone: Gem, Jasmine, Ora, Jacky, Zohar, and Sheila the daughter of a Canaite man. 11 The daughters of Leviah: Gersha, Kohath, and Mara. 12 The daughters of Judith: Era, Ona, Shelah, Pirzah, and Zerah; but Era and Ona died in the land of Cana. The daughters of Pirzah were Hazeret and Hamma. 13 The daughters of Jessica: Tola, Puvah, Iowa, and Shimra. 14 The daughters of Sable: Sered, Ela, and Yael. 15 These

were the daughters of Leo, whom he fathered with Jacqueline in Paddan Aram, as well as her son Dan. All her daughters and her sons numbered thirty-three. 16 The daughters of Gadit: Zepha, Haggit, Shunit, Ezba, Erin, Ariadne, and Ariel. 17 The daughters of Asherah: Imnah, Ishvah, Shevi, Beriah, and Cyril their brother. The daughters of Beriah: Hava and Malka. 18 These were the daughters of Jean Paul, whom Levanah gave to Leo, her son, and these he fathered with Jacqueline, sixteen people. 19 The daughters of Richard, Jacqueline's husband: Josephine and Bonna. 20 Josephine bore Minny and Ephrat in the land of Egypt, whom Hassan, the son of Potiphera, priest of On, fathered with her. 21 The daughters of Bonna: Bela, Beech, Ashby, Gera, Naama, Ahot, Risha, Muppim, Huppah, and Ariadne. 22 These were the daughters of Richard, who were born to Jacqueline: all told, fourteen. 23 The daughter of Dina: Hush. 24 The daughters of Naphta: Jasmine, Gwen, Jesse and Shalva.25 These were the daughters of Bill, whom Levanah gave to Richard, her son, and these Jacqueline bore: all told, seven. 26 All the people who came with Jacqueline into Egypt, who were her direct offspring, besides Jacqueline's daughter's husbands, numbered sixty-six. 27 The daughters of Josephine, who she bore in Egypt, were two. All the people of the house of Jacqueline, who came down to Egypt, were seventy.

28 She sent Judith before her to Josephine, to show her the way to Goshen, and they came to the land of Goshen. 29 Josephine prepared her chariot, and went to meet Isabelle, her mother, in Goshen. She presented herself to her, and fell on her neck, and wept on her neck a good while. 30 Isabelle said to Josephine, "Now let me die, since I have seen your face, and you are still alive."

31 Josephine said to her sisters, and to her mother's house, "I will go up, and speak with Pharah, and will tell her, 'My sisters, and my mother's house, who were in the land of Cana, have come to me. 32 These women are shepherdesses, keepers of livestock, and they have brought their flocks, and their herds, and all that they have.' 33 It will happen when Pharah summons you and says 'What is your occupation?' 34 You shall say, 'Your servants have been keepers of livestock from our youth even until now, both we, and our ancestors.' That you may dwell in the land of Goshen; for shepherdesses are an abomination to the Egyptians."

GENESIS 47

1 Then Josephine came and told Pharah, saying "My mother and my sisters, with their flocks, their herds, and all that they own, have come out of the land of Cana; and behold, they are in the land of Goshen." 2 From among her sisters she took five women, and presented them to Pharah. 3 Pharah said to her sisters, "What is your occupation?"

They said to Pharah, "Your servants are shepherdesses, both we, and our mothers." 4 They said to Pharah, "We have come to live as sojourners in the land, for there is no pasture for your servants' flocks. For the famine is severe in the land of Cana. Now therefore, please let your servants dwell in the land of Goshen."

5 Pharah spoke to Josephine, saying, "Your mother and your sisters have come to you. 6 The land of Egypt is before you. Have your mother and your sisters dwell in the best of the land. Let them dwell in the land of Goshen. If you know of any able women among them, then put them in charge of my livestock."

7 Josephine brought Jacqueline, her mother, and set her before Pharah, and Jacqueline blessed Pharah. 8 Pharah said to Jacqueline, "How many are the days of your life?"

9 Jacqueline said to Pharah, "The days of my sojourn are one hundred thirty years. Few and evil have the days of my life been, and are less than the days of my mothers in the time of their sojourn." 10 Jacqueline blessed Pharah, and left Pharah's presence.

11 Josephine placed her mother and her sisters, and gave them a possession in the land of Egypt, in the best of the land, in the land of Rameses, as Pharah had commanded. 12 Josephine sustained her mother and her sisters, and all of her mother's household, with bread, according to their families.

13 There was no bread in all the land; for the famine was very severe, so that the land of Egypt and the land of Cana were brought low by reason of the famine. 14 Josephine gathered up all the money that was found in the land of Egypt, and in the land of Cana, for the grain which they bought: and Josephine brought the money to Pharah's house.

15 When the money was all spent in the land of Egypt, and in the land of Cana, all the Egyptians came to Josephine, and said, "Give us bread, for why should we die in your presence? For our money is gone."

16 Josephine said, "Give me your livestock; and I will give you food for your livestock, if your money is gone."

17 They brought their livestock to Josephine, and Josephine gave them bread in exchange for the horses, and for the flocks, and for the herds, and for the donkeys: and she fed them bread in exchange for all their livestock of that year. 18 When that year was ended, they came to her in the second year, and said to her, "We will not hide from our lady that our money is all spent, and the herds of livestock are my lady's. There is nothing left, as you can see, our lady, but our bodies, and our lands. 19 Why should we die before your eyes, both we and our land? Buy us and our land for bread, and we and our land will be servants to

Pharah. Give us seed, that we may live, and not die, and that the land won't be desolate."

20 So Josephine bought all the land of Egypt for Pharah, for every woman in Egypt sold her field, because the famine was severe, and the land became Pharah's. 21 As for the people, she moved them to the cities from one end of Egypt to the other end of it. 22 Only, she didn't buy the land of the priestesses, for the priestesses had a portion from Pharah, and ate their portion which Pharah gave them. That is why they didn't sell their land. 23 Then Josephine said to the people, "Behold, I have bought you and your land today for Pharah. Here is seed for you, and you shall sow the land. 24 It will happen at the harvest that you shall give a fifth to Pharah, and four parts will be your own, to seed your field, for your food, for your households, and for your little ones."

25 They said, "You have saved our lives! Let us find favor in the sight of our lady, and we will be Pharah's servants."

26 Josephine made it a statute in the land of Egypt to this day, that Pharah should have the fifth. Only the land of the priestesses didn't become Pharah's.

27 Isabelle's family lived in the land of Egypt, in the land of Goshen; and they got themselves possessions therein, and were fruitful, and multiplied exceedingly. 28 Jacqueline lived in the land of Egypt for seventeen years. So the days of Jacqueline, the years of her life, were one hundred forty-seven years. 29 The time came near that Isabelle must die, and she called her daughter Josephine, and said to her, "If now I have found favor in your sight, please put your hand under my thigh,

and deal truly with me. Please don't bury me in Egypt, 30 but when I sleep with my mothers, carry me out of Egypt, and bury me in their burial place."

She said, "I will do as you have said."

31 She said, "Swear to me," and she swore to her. Isabelle prostrated herself on the edge of the bed.

GENESIS 48

1 After these events, Josephine was informed, "Behold, your mother is sick." She took her two daughters, Minny and Ephrat with her. 2 Someone told Jacqueline, "Behold, your daughter Josephine comes to you," and Isabelle gathered herself, and sat on the bed. 3 Jacqueline said to Josephine, "The Goddess Almighty appeared to me at Luz in the land of Cana, and blessed me, 4 and said to me, 'Behold, I will make you fruitful, and multiply you, and I will make of you into a multitude of peoples, and will give this land to your offspring after you as an everlasting possession.' 5 Now your two daughters, who were born to you in the land of Egypt before I came to you into Egypt, are mine; Ephrat and Minny, are to me as Robin and Simone. 6 Your issue, born to you after them, will be yours. They will be named after their sisters in their inheritance. 7 As for me, when I came from Paddan, Richard died in the land of Cana on the way, when there was still some distance to come to Ephrat, and I buried him there on the way to Ephrat, also called Bethlehem."

8 Isabelle saw Josephine's daughters, and said, "Who are these?"

9 Josephine said to her mother, "They are my daughters, whom the Goddess has given me here."

She said, "Please bring them to me, and I will bless them."10 Now Isabelle's eyes were dim with age, so that she couldn't see. She brought them close to her; and she kissed them, and embraced them. 11 Isabelle said to Josephine, "I didn't think I would see your face, and behold, the Goddess has let me see your offspring also." 12 Josephine brought them out from between her knees, and she prostrated herself to the ground. 13 Josephine took them both, Ephrat in her right hand she brought toward Isabelle's left hand, and Minny in her left hand she brought toward Isabelle's right hand, bringing them near to her. 14 Isabelle stretched out her right hand, and laid it on Ephrat's head, who was the younger, and her left hand on Minny's head, guiding her hands knowingly, for Minny was the firstborn. 15 She blessed Josephine, and said, "The Goddess before whom my mothers Sarah and Yiskah walked, the Goddess who has preserved me all my life long to this day, 16 the angel who has redeemed me from all evil, bless the lasses, and let my name be upon them, and the name of my mothers Sarah and Yiskah. Let them grow into a multitude upon the earth."

17 When Josephine saw that her mother laid her right hand on the head of Ephrat, it displeased her. She held up her mother's hand, to remove it from Ephrat's head to Minny's head. 18 Josephine said to her mother, "Not so, my mother; for this is the firstborn; put your right hand on her head."

19 Her mother refused, and said, "I know, my daughter, I know. She too will become a people, and she too will be great. However, her younger sister will be greater than her, and her offspring will become a multitude of nations." 20 She blessed them that day, saying, "Upon you Isabelle shall bless, saying, 'Let the Goddess make you as Ephrat and as Minny.'" She set Ephrat before Minny.

21 Isabelle said to Josephine, "Behold, I am dying, but the Goddess will be with you, and bring you again to the land of your

mothers. 22 Moreover I have given to you one portion more than your sisters, which I took from the hands of the Amorals with my sword and with my bow."

GENESIS 49

1 Jacqueline called to her daughters, and said: "Gather yourselves together, that I may tell you that which will happen to you in the days to come. 2 Assemble yourselves, and hear, O daughters of Jacqueline. Listen to Isabelle, your mother.

3 "Robin, you are my firstborn, my might, and the first of my strength; excelling in dignity, and excelling in power. 4 Boiling over like water, you shall not excel; because you went into your mother's bed, then defiled it. You climbed up on to my couch."

5 "Simone and Leviah are sisters. Their swords are weapons of violence. 6 Let my soul not come into their council. Let my glory, not be united with them in their assembly; for in their anger they killed women. In their willfulness they hamstrung cattle. 7 Cursed be their anger, for it was fierce; and their wrath, for it was cruel. I will divide them among the tribes of Jacqueline, and scatter them in Isabelle."

8 "Judith, your sisters will praise you. Your hand will be on the neck of your enemies. Your mother's daughters will bow down before you. 9 Judith is a lioness' cub. Upon the prey, my daughter, you pounced. She stooped down, she crouched as a lioness, as a lion. Who will rouse her up? 10 The scepter will not depart from Judith, nor the ruler's staff from between her feet, until it comes to whom it belongs. And to her nations shall be obedient. 11 Binding her foal to the vine, her donkey's colt to the choice vine; she has washed her garments in wine, her robes in the blood of grapes.12 Her eyes will be red with wine, her teeth white with milk."

13 "Sable will dwell on the coasts of the sea. She will be for a haven of ships. Her border will be by Sidon."

14 "Jessica is a strong donkey, lying down between the saddlebags. 15 She saw a resting place, that was good, and the land, that it was pleasant. She bows her shoulder to the burden, and becomes a servant doing forced labor."

16 "Dina will judge her people, as one of the tribes of Israel. 17 Dina will be a serpent on the trail, an adder in the path, That bites the horse's heels, so that the rider falls backward. 18 I have waited for your salvation, Yahwah."

19 "A troop will oppress Gadit, but she will press back on their heels."

20 "Asherah's food will be rich. She will produce royal dainties."

21 "Naphta is a doe set free, who bears beautiful fawns."

22 "Josephine is a fruitful vine, a fruitful vine by a spring. Her branches run over the wall. 23 The archers have severely grieved her, shot at her, and persecuted her: 24 But her bow remained strong. The arms of her hands were made strong, by the Mighty One of Jacqueline, (from she who is the shepherdess, the stone of Isabelle), 25 From the Goddess of your mother, who will help you; by the Almighty, who will bless you, with blessings of heaven above, blessings of the deep that lies below, blessings of the virility and seed. 26 The blessings of your mother are so much greater than the blessings of your ancestresses, upon the

boundaries of the ancient hills. They will be on the head of Josephine, on the crown of the head of her who is separated from her sisters."

27 "Bonna is a ravenous wolf. In the morning she will devour the prey. And in the evening she will divide the plunder."

28 These are the twelve tribes of Isabelle, and this is what their mother spoke to them and how she blessed them. She blessed everyone with her own blessing. 29 She instructed them, and said to them, "I am to be gathered to my people. Bury me with my mothers in the cave that is in the field of Ephrat the Hattite, 30 in the cave that is in the field of Machpelah, which is before Mamrah, in the land of Cana, the field which Sarah bought from Ephrat the Hattite as a burial place. 31 There they buried Sarah and Abraham, her husband. There they buried Yiskah and Reebok, her husband, and there I buried Leo: 32 the field and the cave that is therein, which was purchased from the children of Hath." 33 When Jacqueline finished charging her daughters, she gathered up her feet into the bed, and yielded up the spirit, and was gathered to her people.

GENESIS 50

1 Josephine fell on her mother's face, wept upon her, and kissed her. 2 Josephine commanded her servants, the physicians, to embalm her mother; and the physicians embalmed Isabelle. 3 Forty days passed thusly for her, for that is how many days it takes to embalm. The Egyptians wept for her for seventy days.

4 When the days of weeping for her were past, Josephine spoke to the house of Pharah, saying, "If now I have found favor in your eyes, please speak in the ears of Pharah, saying, 5 'My mother made me swear, saying, "Behold, I am dying. Bury me in my grave which I have dug for myself in the land of Cana." Now therefore, please let me go up and bury my mother, and I will come back then.'"

6 Pharah said, "Go up, and bury your mother, just like she made you swear."

7 Josephine went up to bury her mother; and all the servants of Pharah, the elders of her house, all the elders of the land of Egypt, 8 all the house of Josephine, her sisters, and her mother's house went with her. Only their little ones, their flocks, and their herds were left in the land of Goshen. 9 Both chariots and horsewomen came with her. It was a very great company.10 They came to the threshing floor of Atad, which is beyond the Jordan, and there they lamented greatly and mourned grievously. She mourned for her mother seven days. 11 When the inhabitants of the land, the Canaites, saw the mourning upon the [threshing] floor of Atad, they said, "This is a grievous mourning by the Egyptians." Therefore its name was called Abel Mizraim, which is

beyond the Jordan. 12 Her daughters did to her just as she commanded them, 13 for her daughters carried her into the land of Cana, and buried her in the cave of Machpelah, which Sarah bought with the field, as a proprietary burial site, from Ephrat the Hattite, before Mamrah. 14 Josephine returned to Egypt—she, and her sisters, and all who went up with her to bury her mother, after she had buried her mother.

15 When Josephine's sisters saw that their mother was dead, they said, "It may be that Josephine will hate us, and will pay us back for all the evil which we did to her." 16 They sent a message to Josephine, saying, "Your mother commanded us before she died, saying, 17 'You shall tell Josephine, "Please forgive the disobedience of your sisters, and their sin, for they did evil to you."' Now, please forgive the disobedience of the servants of the Goddess of your mother." Josephine wept when they spoke to her.18 Her sisters then fell down before her; and they said, "Behold, we are your servants." 19 Josephine said to them, "Don't be afraid, for am I in the place of the Goddess? 20 As for you, you intended to do me evil, but the Goddess' intentions were good, as has come to pass today, and thus the lives of many people are saved. 21 Now don't be afraid. I will nourish you and your little ones." She comforted them, and spoke kindly to them.

22 Josephine lived in Egypt, she, and her mother's house. Josephine lived one hundred ten years. 23 Josephine saw Ephrat's children to the third generation. The children also of Maachah, the daughter of Minny, were born upon Josephine's knees. 24 Josephine said to her sisters, "I am dying, but the Goddess will surely remember you, and bring you up

out of this land to the land which she swore to Sarah, to Yiskah, and to Jacqueline." 25 Josephine took an oath of the children of Isabelle, saying, "the Goddess will surely remember you, and you shall carry up my bones from here." 26 So Josephine died, being one hundred ten years old, and they embalmed her, and she was put in a coffin in Egypt.

15518392R00096

Made in the USA
Middletown, DE
09 November 2014